D0150492

Set Your Hearts
on the Greatest Gift

Morton Kelsey

Set Your Hearts on the Greatest Gift

Living the Art of Christian Love

New City Press

Dedication

To Clara Smith Kleintop, a special early care giver
To Barbara, my wife of fifty-one years, who made the story possible
To my children, Myra, Chip and John, who are still teaching me
To John Neary, who helped me tell the story

Published in the United States by New City Press
202 Cardinal Rd., Hyde Park, NY 12538
©1996 Morton Kelsey

Cover design: Ave Center, Loppiano, Italy

Library of Congress Cataloging-in-Publication Data:

Kelsey, Morton T.
    Set your hearts on the greatest gift: living the art of Christian
love / Morton Kelsey.

    Includes bibliographical references.
    ISBN 1-56548-043-0 (pbk.)
    1. God—Love.   2. God—Worship and love.   3. Love—Religious
aspects—Christianity.   4. Kelsey, Morton T.   I. Title.
BT140.K46   1996
231'.6—dc20   95-34531

Printed in the United States of America

Contents

Growing in Love

This book is a very personal account of how we can grow in the art of Christian love. Every one of the great religions of humankind emphasizes the importance of love as our guide and goal of the spiritual journey. Most philosophers have come to the same conclusion. No one, however, has stated this truth more clearly than Jesus of Nazareth. By the stories that he told and by the story that he lived, Jesus brought a new depth and meaning to the world "love," *agape* in the Greek of the New Testament. Jesus began his ministry by proclaiming that the kingdom of heaven and of love is at hand and that we can begin to share in it now and eternally. This was the essence of his message. Starting with Paul, the Christian fellowship fed the ancient world with love by teaching and living that love. Within three hundred years that heroic and ever-growing fellowship took control of the Roman Empire that was trying to destroy the Christian Church.

Each of us has a unique pathway of growing into the fullness of love. I have listened to many people who were seeking to grow spiritually, to become closer to the Holy One. I have come to see that it is necessary to learn to love other human beings if we are to become closer to the divine Lover. Love and true spirituality are two sides of the same coin, two poles of the same magnet.

This book contains a group of connected stories about how we can better love one another and the divine Lover. Most of us human beings are more touched by story than by logic. Lecturing around the world I have found that when I shared the story of Jesus' life and his stories and have shown how theses stories related to the stories of our own lives, people have heard more clearly the incredible message of the Creator's love for us. We are called to love one another as we are loved by God, who created this very universe so that we might be caught up in the mystery and power of love.

In my life there have been real difficulties and real joys, and the right person has been sent my way when my need was greatest. The greatest source of love and honesty in my life has been Barbara, my wife of fifty-one years. We met through a strange combination of "coincidences." Each of my children have given me new insights into love that no one else could have been in a position to provide. In addition grace has provided me a host of friends who have stuck with me through storms and fair weather. One of them with literary expertise edited this manuscript for me.

With this book I tell the story of what can happen when we set our hearts on the greatest gift.

The Journey Home

At Christmas time many years ago, a friend wrote me one of the most magnificent letters I have ever received. In it he asked the question: "Why does the mystical experience, the direct experience of God, seem to fill religious history, but seem absent for most people in our time?" He then went on to write these words:

> I slowly began to think that the answer to this might be similar to many questions of like nature — that we are not so very different from medieval women and men or those of the time of Christ as we think. Only the form or manner of expression changes, not the essence. I think that the mystical experience, the unitive vision, is as much among us and as available as it ever has been. The finding takes only simplicity and directness. The simplicity yields that most simple statement possible from scripture: God is love. Directness takes one to search for the experience of love within one's own life.

What he wrote is indeed very simple — we can find the splendor of God only as we come to know what love is concretely in our own lives, and however it expresses itself in us. Yet most of us are afraid to truly love. My friend's letter went on:

> With love there are no defenses, and one may be hurt deeply, again and again. And then, as we truly love, the power and majesty and splendor of God come upon us, and this is not always gentle or easy to take. The splendor of God has little in common with a Sunday School picnic, or the parlor game of *love*. When we allow ourselves to love specifically, fully and consciously, concretely and in depth,

9

then we are at the very edge of Love itself (love with a capital L), of the mystical splendor of God. From many sources we are told that the mystical splendor of God will first burn us down, melt away all that does not belong to us, shear us of everything that we thought necessary for life, destroy everything that is not pure gold in us. This is not an easy experience. But it is the most important one in life, and probably the only human experience that is eternal and cannot be lost in the shuffle.

Too often we like to talk about love and deal with it philosophically or by writing poetry about it, when the important thing is to live it. As Laurens Van der Post has clearly expressed in his novel *The Seed and the Sower*, love has to be brought down to earth by women and men who exemplify and manifest it. The task of the very real human being, he says, is to make the universal specific, the general concrete. The job of the Christian, then, is to allow Love to act in and through us in *specific action, in concrete kindness and loving deed.*[1]

My friend's words struck their mark. I knew that they were speaking of the essence of Christianity. Had I received them earlier, however, I would not have understood them. I had been studying Christianity and trying to share the Christian message for over twenty years, but I had not seen that human caring and a fellowship with the God of love are opposite sides of the same coin. And then I finally had an experience that opened my eyes, my mind, my heart and soul to the secret of the Christian gospel. Why had it taken so long?

As I was growing up, I did not experience unconditional love and acceptance from my family or teachers. Then, when I was in my early twenties, my mother, the person who gave me the greatest amount of love died. Not long before she died, she uttered these paradoxical words:

Morton, if you had turned against me or neglected me in these last months, it would have served me right for neglecting you as a child.

Only within the last year have I discovered the full significance of those words; later I will describe the experience of grace that enabled me to understand that statement.

Shortly after my mother's death, I went to study philosophy in the graduate school at Princeton University. There I encountered a cynical agnosticism and atheism that cleaned away any shred of Christian belief left over from a hopelessly inadequate religious education. (Ironically, many years later I was to spend some of my best years teaching religious education in the Graduate Department of Education at another fine university, the University of Notre Dame du Lac, near South Bend, Indiana.²) My learned professors at Princeton scorned Christianity and confessed that they could not understand why the writing of Plato retained such life and power. They had no place in their thinking for Plato's basic idea that love leads to God. I realized, while at Princeton, that I was in a very dark wood and that I might be lost forever if I did not find some meaning. I left graduate study and found a job teaching fourth, fifth and sixth grades at a military academy.

Grace intervened in the form of a very wise and caring priest in a little country parish in upstate New York. He invited me again and again to have Sunday dinner with him and his family. *He listened to me*; he never judged my doubts, and he was not shocked or afraid of my lostness. He showed me that Christians counted some very intelligent people among their ranks, and he suggested that I go to seminary to find out for myself. I entered the Episcopal Theological School in Cambridge, Massachusetts, the next fall and worked very hard. I learned all the great stories of the Old and New Testaments; I soon knew the Bible from cover to cover. I also learned enough Greek and Hebrew so that I could translate any puzzling passages. I was struck by the courage of the early Christians in the face of persecution. I was fascinated by the intellectual leaders of the Church, who laid a foundation for vital Christian teaching, healing, prayer and love. In addition, I read theology and ethics.

However, the atmosphere in seminary was competitive and cold. The professors were distant, and they feared that students might have entered seminary to avoid the draft. No classes were provided in how to pray or love or listen, in how to teach or relate to those who would be our future congregations. The statement that we "could love people without liking them" didn't sound right to me even coming from the lips of a revered old bishop in one of our seminars. Most sadly I learned almost nothing about the meaning and practice of Christian love.

Twenty years in three growing parishes did not teach me much more about love and caring. I found that lay people responded to the clergy when they called, but I found jealousy, malicious gossip and egotism both in the congregation and among ministers. Lay people did not realize their need to love one another. Although I felt that it was wrong to have the same lack of caring among Christians as among those who were frankly agnostic or atheists, I didn't make much headway in bringing a more caring spirit to the churches I served. I realized I must be missing something: I knew that love was *one* important part of the good news of Jesus of Nazareth and of the Holy One of Israel. But I hadn't the vaguest idea that love was truly the center, foundation and goal of the Christian life. I had looked at love only with my head, not with my heart. And then I had an experience of God's transforming and healing love.

In the Silence of a Plane

My experience occurred when I was on a plane flying across the continent, heading home after presenting my first large conference about developing the spiritual life. The tiny plane swooped down into one little airfield after another, giving passengers an immanent sense of eternity. My journal was open in my lap. As I was writing, I began reflecting on the four days I had spent speaking to large groups of people in Goldsboro, North Carolina. I usually write in my journal when I wish to focus my attention in prayer, in order to listen to the Spirit. I asked the Spirit: "Were my presentations effective? Had I been of any real value to the people? How did I do?"

As I quieted down, the silence became deafening. I realized that the plane was flying very close to the home of my brother and only sibling. He and I had merely a Christmas-card relationship; we had never been close. I suddenly realized that there was no hope for our relationship unless I made all the overtures. I also realized that I had given up hope and had stopped trying to reach out with caring. This seemed like a strange answer to the question I had posed the Spirit. It made me uncomfortable.

Then I became aware that the next lap of my journey would take me over a section of the country in which my father lived. My father never seemed to value what I did or who I was. He had not read my newly published book, which I had sent him. He was married to a woman I viewed as a perfect example of a fairy-tale stepmother. Although I wrote to my father occasionally and visited when necessary, I had come to feel that any real communication with him was impossible, and I had ceased trying to relate to him in any real way.

And then another realization swept over me: I had planned this trip home with an extended stop-over in Phoenix, Arizona, because of yet another strained relationship in my life. My daughter, with whom I'd had a rocky relationship since she entered her early teens, was attending college in Phoenix, and a friend with several daughters had suggested that I might improve our relationship if I visited her on her own turf. I had phoned her to tell her that I had arranged a five-hour stopover in Phoenix just to see her. (I am glad that I did not know her reaction to my call until after the visit. She asked her best friend: "What will I do with my father for five hours?" Also she was not happy with her position as a minister's daughter, considering the lack of affluence that went with that profession.)

I was shocked as I wrote all this in my journal. I had certainly not given my family unconditional love. With the silence only broken by the roar of jet engines, the following words bubbled up out of the depth of me, and I wrote them down:

O Divine Master,
   grant that I may not so much seek
   to be consoled —
      as to console,
   to be understood —
      as to understand,
   to be loved —
      as to love.

These words spoke profoundly to my situation; I knew they were true. But I did not know the source of the words — I did not recall having heard them before. If I had heard them, they had been recorded on a deep mysterious level of my being and were allowed to rise at the right moment. When I returned home, I tried to find these words in the Bible using my concordance, but they were not there. I do not recall how I found them. They were the central section of a prayer very dear to Francis of Assisi. Twenty years before I had read a life of Francis. I had been impressed by this saint. He had followed the way of Jesus as fully as any person in history.

I did not generate these words and their message: They crashed into my consciousness unbidden. I wrote them down. As I meditated on these words in the quiet, three new insights, revelations, came to me. I believe they emerged from the depth of my being, that part of me in touch with the divine Spirit. The psalmist did not ask to be given the Holy Spirit, but only that it might not be taken away (Ps 51:11).

First of all I saw clearly for the first time that I had been more interested in being consoled, understood and loved than in giving other people consolation, understanding and love, and particularly within my own family. I was expecting my brother and father, stepmother and daughter, wife and friends to take care of my feelings, to care for me. If they didn't, then the relationship had failed, and I needed to do nothing to mend it.

Then it became clear to me that most of us human beings are more interested in being taken care of, in being loved, consoled and understood than in reaching out with these gifts to others — even those closest to us. How often parents are trying to get their children to satisfy their needs for sympathy and affection. Many adult children are still often looking to their parents for support and strength and caring without considering their parents' needs.

I then understood why in my years of preaching about love and caring I had made so little change in the congregations that I served. These people were just like me. They could see that I was not motivated by unconditional love, that I was seeking approval and concern from them as well as my family. How frequently we complain: "She did not speak to me or invite me to her party." "He did not consider me as a member of his group or did not pay proper attention to me." Our feelings are so easily hurt from a variety of reasons, ranging from an imagined slur to an angry word or nasty action. Most of us most of the time want to be treated like a Ming vase.

So much of this complaining and hurt feelings would cease in our social and religious groups if we took seriously and internalized these words of Francis. How could our wounded feelings persist if we were intent on bringing consolation and understanding to others instead of being overly concerned about our own? It would be practically impossible. We can seldom lead others further than we ourselves have traveled. I needed to change if I was to minister effectively.

Almost as soon as I had written down this insight about the practical importance of unconditional love, another insight forced its way into my consciousness. I saw clearly that these words of Francis pointed the way not only to religious maturity and effectiveness but to emotional, psychological maturity as well. I had been studying psychology in an attempt to understand myself and those around me. This prayer opened my understanding to a new truth: Emotional maturity only *begins* to take place in us when we become more interested in giving of ourselves than in just receiving. Children need to be showered with love and understanding from the moment that they emerge from the womb. They only learn to love and care by being loved and cared for. Lack of love and human touch can even result in death. The death rate of babies under a year of age in spotlessly clean orphanages was nearly thirty-five percent in the early years of the twentieth century. They died of a strange disease called *marasmus*, a Greek word that means slowly wasting away. Then Dr. René Spitz brought women into a foundling home. Their task was mainly to pick up the babies, hold and love them. The death rate dropped to ten percent within a year at that home.

Children need and desire to be loved and held. They are interested only in themselves. This is a natural stage of development. To pass from childhood and childishness to adulthood, however, requires a shift from merely receiving loving and understanding to giving caring concern to others. The essential mark of a mature adult is the ability to give love, expecting nothing in return. Until we can give love and understanding — without any strings attached — we still remain emotional children no matter how physically or intellectually grown up we are. Until we are not more interested in giving love rather than just receiving it, we are still immature, self-centered children. It was the words of this prayer that pulled together my psychological study and showed me the direction my life should take.[3] I realized I still had a lot of maturing to do.

As I was mulling over the second new realization, a third insight emerged from the depth of me, the most profound of all. Love was not only the way to better relationships or a guide to genuine maturity, it was the way of Francis, of the Holy Spirit, of Jesus of Nazareth, of God and the fellowship of heaven. Indeed, in the Gospels the word "heaven" was often used in place of the Holy One of Israel. The pieces of the puzzle came together. Love was the soul and center of all reality. *God is love.* The divine Lover created the universe in order to express love. Then the Holy One of Israel called Abraham to found a chosen people. When people did not respond to the servants God inspired, God loved them so much that the divine One became flesh in Jesus as a baby in a stable. Jesus came among us to show God's love for all people.

Jesus began his ministry by declaring that the reign of God was at hand, the love of heaven was available to human beings now. Jesus showed his love by giving dignity to every person, giving hope to the broken, neglected and forgotten. He healed those without hope and also the emotionally and physically sick, because he loved them and was offended by the powers that marred human beings. He showed his love to his disciples by washing their feet. He provided a last supper so that they could experience his continued presence among them when he was gone. Jesus loved them to the end. He met evil head on to ransom humankind from evil and the Evil One. He was crucified, died and was buried, and then he loved so much that he rose from the dead. He returned to his broken disciples and shaped them into a courageous and victorious company that conquered the empire which had destroyed him. In his ascension he became available to all space and time. Jesus sent the paraclete, the Holy Spirit, the loving defender, to be with us and to lead us beyond evil to eternal life in the kingdom of love.

The essential nature of the Creator, Redeemer and Sanctifier, the Trinity, is love. The Divine wanted to pour that love out upon the human race. Our task was and is to be open to this love and then to share it with all those around us. Those who fail to do this are imperfect in their following of the risen Jesus.

I saw that the real following of Jesus of Nazareth begins when we grasp the fact that it is more important to console and understand and love than it was to stretch our hands to grasp this kind of caring. It is not easy to give up our desire for satisfaction, attention and love. Indeed when we begin to give up those desires, something new comes to birth in us. As we proceed upon this way, we lose our lives in order to gain them. As we live out Francis' prayer, we die and rise again. When we try to live by this one little prayer, the whole gospel opens up. It comes to life.

Suddenly the way of the risen Jesus begins to make sense. The Bible, the creed, the Lord's Prayer, the ministry of Jesus, his resurrection and ascension, the eucharist, eternal life and the amazing history of the early Church make sense. The whole gospel begins to open up like a tightly closed bud into the glorious white rose that Dante saw in his vision of heaven. Love is essential to every aspect of real Christianity, just as our life's blood sustains and heals every part of the human body. Our bodies die when the blood ceases flowing through us.

A Confirming Experience

At this point in my reflection the plane landed in Phoenix, Arizona. My daughter met me in her friend's car. It was lunch time. I asked her where she would like to go for lunch — any place in Phoenix. She was so surprised by this kind of invitation from her minister father that she couldn't think of a place to go. Finally I took her to one of the loveliest resort hotels where we sat beside the pool, and the waiters hovered over us. I was focusing my entire attention on her, listening and responding to her.

As we talked at our leisurely lunch, she sensed that something had changed in father. Timidly she asked if I would like to go shopping in the Thomas Mall that afternoon. Frankly, that was not my idea of a balmy February in Phoenix. Before I answered I paused and remembered that I was there to love and console and understand. How infinitely important it is to pause and consider that our goal is love before we speak or act. So I answered, "Myra, I would love to go shopping with you in the Thomas Mall." I was not lying. I put aside my egotism and served love. Love is both our feeling and our consciously willed action.

We drove to the Mall. It was huge; we walked up and back, up and back in the air-conditioned shopping center. Since loving was my goal, I was watching my daughter and her reactions. I noted twice in our walking, her pace slackened in front of a certain shoe store. The next time that we came to the store, I stopped. I noted that her eyes lighted upon a pair of yellow shoes. I said, "Myra, would you like to try on those shoes?" She thought that was a nice idea. Naturally, they fitted perfectly. (That is known in theological language as "divine providence.") There was a yellow bag to match. I asked her if she would like it, adding, "My dear, this does not come out of your allowance; this is a gift." A pure gift in religious language is called grace.

Something happened that day between my daughter and me. I realized how much I really cared about her. She realized that I could be interested in her. She could forgive my previous behavior. No longer was it, "What will I do with father for five hours?" but, "Why don't you come more often and stay longer?" She knew now that I could see her for herself. The size of the gift was not what counted. It could have been a chocolate sundae or an ice-cream cone. What mattered was that I tried to love and understand. It has remained this way except when I have fallen back into unconsciousness and not acted in love.

I call this the sacrament of the yellow shoes.

Francis of Assisi — The Example

As soon as I returned home and found the source of the words that struck me so deeply, I began to study the one who used them. These words had opened a new dimension of reality to me. The most amazing thing about them is that Francis actually lived the words of the prayer that bears his name. Perhaps this is why they ring with such an authentic note, why they are so real. Francis of Assisi modeled his life on that of Jesus of Nazareth more fully than anyone had in centuries. So magnetic was the power of his love that people were drawn to him from every walk of life, the rich and poor, the illiterate and the learned. Many were transformed. All were welcomed. Thousands followed him. Out of sheer necessity, he founded the Franciscan orders for men and women so these people had an opportunity to embrace a truly meaningful life. In the early days of the thirteenth century, the Church had lost its fire; it was dormant and cynical. In less than twenty years Francis revitalized Christianity. This new life flowered in a new depth of prayer and worship, in the great Christian art and in the magnificent Gothic churches that were a symbol of

the human reaching up to the divine Lover. This transformation
was ignited and driven by the quality of divine love that flowed
through Francis. Great leaders arose among the Franciscans to
continue the spirit of Francis that continues in some places until
today.

He had religious experience contemplating the crucifix. He
knew that Jesus had called him to rebuild his Church and to bring
a message of compassion and love back to the Church and the
world. The stories of his love are innumerable. One tells of
Francis' reply to a brother who asked with malicious sarcasm and
envy, "Why did God pick you?" The answer came back, "I guess
Jesus picked the humblest and most insignificant so his glory
would show through without question." Francis ministered to
beggars, lepers, the broken and forgotten, and he also ministered
to the nobility and kings. He even tried to convert the Sultan in
Egypt. It is said that even animals were drawn to him and that
he preached to the birds. He was far more than an activist. He
touched the deepest springs of the holy and from these came
visions and spiritual experiences of the most uncanny kind.

What is even more significant, Francis had not always lived in
this loving and creative manner. As a youth he was confused and
lost, and so he gives hope to the lost and broken of all times.
Transformation in love wipes out the past. Love covers a multitude of sins (Pt 4:7). His life says it is never too late. Francis died
at the age of forty-four, but he had changed his world and our
world.

Ever since his death, his example has continued to change lives
—millions of them. The words that came to me on the plane were
the central portion of what he called "A Simple Prayer."

And what happens when we try to be more interested in loving
and consoling and understanding than in being loved, consoled
and understood? We become instruments of God's peace in the
world:

> Where there is hatred,
> we sow love,

where there is injury,
  we bestow pardon,
where there is doubt,
  we bring faith,
where there is despair,
  we bring hope,
where there is darkness,
  we shed light,
where there is weakness,
  we inspire strength,
and where there is sadness,
  we bring joy.

All this flows naturally from the life which seeks to give rather than to receive. Such a life spreads love, pardon, faith, hope, light, strength and joy. Inevitably!

And inwardly, when we live this way, we are filled, pardoned and given eternal life, for it is in giving that we receive; it is in pardoning that we are pardoned; it is in dying that we are born to eternal life.

Love breeds love. This is the only way that it spreads out into the world. In other words, in this world love is its own source. It cannot be reached through will or intellect or understanding. It springs out of the total reality of a human being—body, soul and mind that has been touched directly by divine Love or from another person who has been touched by the Holy One and shares that love with us. Love that is merely rationally willed and does not spring out of the heart is really no love at all. It is only, in Berdyaev's words, "glassy Christian love" which has little transforming power. He believed that one of the failures of much of modern Christianity is that it rationalizes love and does not provide the warm and caring community that nurtures people in the kind of love that Francis exemplifies. One reason that the pagan world embraced Christianity was the love that Christians dying in the arena showed to one another and the pagans. Commenting on this, one scholar wrote that when modern Christians no longer show that kind of love, the world will become pagan once again.

When St. Perpetua was led into the arena to be torn apart by wild beasts, her jailers exclaimed: "[Unlike most people] you are not cursing us or the informer who betrayed you or the judge who sentenced you to this death." She replied with kindness that she did not wish to add to the burdens they already carried. She wanted rather to pray for them that they might know God's love. Actions like this converted the pagan world.

The Boundless, Many-Faceted Jewel of Love

I was in my fifties when my only brother died unexpectedly. He was six years older than I. His family was unable to reach me or my family. He had been buried before we knew of his death. Shortly after this I set out on a lecturing trip. In the plane I realized a heaviness and darkness which settled upon me. I took out my journal to reflect. I realized that I had not faced this death of my only sibling. I was now the oldest one of my immediate family, the next one who might be struck down. I also realized that I was afraid of death, afraid of the image of death reaching out to touch me with a bony finger and take me with him also. I also realized that I had no power over death. In my journal I cried out to this ominous and deadly figure:

"Why don't you take me, do your deed?
A silver filament is all that holds you back. . . .
You do not move. You cannot move?
Oh, you can't cross over? It frightens you?
You, Death, are afraid and tremble?
You have died, have been defeated?"
My eyes become accustomed to the gloom.
The silver thread is more. It is a net,
Let down from heaven. And I look up —
There is a brightness and out of it flow images. . . .
Comforting arms, tears like rain,

Angelic figures, tentacles of light,
A manger and a child, a heavenly
Mother, father, brother, sister,
Lover, friend, ransom, guide
Proclaiming heaven's presence now.
A healing shepherd, One resurrected
From a cross and tomb, endless light,
Pouring out a flood of hope and joy
And peace to friends and seekers.
Within the shining center appeared
A boundless jewel turning one face
And then another. From this there hangs
A net of silver and of gold which stands
Between me and the grinning skull,
Surrounds him as a silken pouch.
A voice like thunder shakes the net.
Shakes heaven, earth and even hell.
"He cannot have you long, this one.
His victory is for the moment only.
And he cannot even have his day
Until the time is ripe and full.
Death has died and so has lost his power.
He risked all and lost. His power's fear.
Only as you fear him can he control.
Only as you're drawn into the net,
Having given up in fear,
As rabbits move toward the snake's hypnotic eye.
Stare him down. Laugh in his face.
I am with you until the end,
With those you love whom death has touched.
They are not lost because they disappear.
Remember me, my child, my beloved.
I am here, always, and with love!"
The thunder rolls away. The rain falls.
I look Death in the face, straight on. I laugh.
He turns and slinks away.[4]

The darkness lifted, and I realized that I had something of value to present to the group of mathematicians who had invited me to come and talk about meditation, prayer, about the experience of the holy. I had been lifted out of the darkness by the Saving One.

This boundless jewel is the many-faceted reality of love and eternal life. Jesus came among us to make this real for us. He usually spoke in parables, in the eternal images of the human soul, so his stories are timeless, as fresh now as when he spoke them. He used many, many different images as he was describing for us the boundlessness of God and Love. One story is so profound and clear that it is often called the gospel within the Gospel. In the following chapter, we shall listen to this story.[5]

The Gospel within the Gospel

Jesus and his disciples were traveling toward Jerusalem for the last time. They were accompanied by a group of faithful women, who took care of their needs. In addition, great crowds of dispossessed common people were following Jesus from town to town; they watched his healing miracles and hung on his every word. Many of these people had been driven from their land by rich landlords, who took over the land when the poor tenants could not repay their loans. These people had to wait in the village squares, looking for someone to hire them.[1] Unable to keep the Jewish ritual law, they were considered sinners by the scribes and Pharisees. Thus, many of Jesus' followers were the down and out, the riff-raff of the time. Others were tax collectors, despised because they were agents of the Romans, who had consolidated their control of Palestine. These people were also considered unclean, because they were in close contact with the Gentile oppressors. Jesus welcomed all these people and ministered to them; he showered the love of heaven upon them.

Social Chaos in Roman Palestine

With the aid of Imperial Rome, Herod Antipas had built great Gentile cities in Sepphoris, five miles from Nazareth and in Tiberias on the Sea of Galilee. Herod was only concerned with the Roman Emperor, who gave him his power, and with the great landowners and the enormously wealthy priestly families, who also gave their basic allegiance to Rome. All of Palestine was in social chaos; unemployment was rife. No one seemed to care about the downtrodden of Israel. It was these desperate people who heard Jesus' message of hope: The kingdom of heaven is at

25

hand. Jesus brought hope to a disinherited and despairing people. However, their religious leaders, the scribes and Pharisees,
did not lift a finger to help them; indeed, these leaders regarded
them as sinners, almost in the same class as Gentiles. The rich,
with the help of a foreign army, were growing richer, and the
poor were growing poorer.[2]

During this last journey to Jerusalem, these dispossessed people gathered around the house where Jesus had slept. A hush fell
upon the crowd as Jesus stepped out and began to speak of the
cost of discipleship, of giving up everything for the kingdom of
heaven. Since many of his listeners had no possessions, they were
not troubled to hear that they had to give up their possessions.
But as the throng continued to grow, a group of scribes and
Pharisees made their way through the mob, and these people
grumbled out loud. Everyone could hear them say to one another: "This fellow actually receives and cordially welcomes
sinners, and he even *eats* with them. He is a dangerous and
wicked man." Then Jesus, looking at the grumblers, spoke four
parables. Each parable told of God's love and concern for all the
lost, for the broken and the oppressed, even for tax collectors.

The Lost Sheep and the Lost Coin

Jesus first told of a sheep lost in the wilderness at night, in
danger of being destroyed by wild beasts. A shepherd searches
through the darkness until he hears the bleating of the frightened
lost one. The shepherd frees the sheep from a thicket and *carries
it home on his own shoulders*. Arriving home, he immediately
invites his friends and neighbors with the urgent invitation:
"Come and rejoice with me. I have found my lost sheep." When
the guests gather, he brings out a wineskin and sweet breads, and
they celebrate his good fortune with him. Jesus ended the story
with a statement that made his meaning very clear: "I tell you
there will be more joy in the kingdom of heaven [in the eternal
fellowship and family of the Holy One of Israel] over one sinner

who repents than over the ninety-nine righteous persons who need no repentance."[3]

Jesus was sharing with the crowd his intimate experience of the Creator, whom Jesus called "Abba." This was an affectionate word that Jewish children used in calling out to their loving fathers; it is closer in English to "Daddy" than to "Father." A friend told me that when he was in a Jewish section of New York, he once heard a lost child calling out, "Abba! Abba!" There was no equally tender Greek word for "Father," so the early Christians continued to use this Aramaic and Hebrew word (used only within the intimacy of the family) as their name for God. Calling God "Abba" implies that the kingdom of heaven is at hand: The loving, tender, caring, eternal Love is seeking all the lost sheep, all the lost human beings, and wishes to find them and carry them home upon the divine shoulders. What good news this was to the lost people who followed Jesus, and what a gentle rebuke to those who were criticizing Jesus.

The crowd was hushed into silence, and then Jesus used another picture — found nowhere else in the gospels — to describe the persistent searching of the Holy One for all of us human beings. Jesus told the story of a Palestinian woman who has worked hard and saved over many years and has finally accumulated ten silver coins. This will be her only resource if she is sick or injured; it is her insurance policy. She is adding her most recent earnings to the other meager savings when she hears the tinkle of one silver coin dropping on the stone floor. She finds her lamp and lights it, and then she begins to sweep the entire floor of the tiny house with great care. At last she finds the lost coin in the corner in which it had rolled. In her joy, the woman calls out to her neighbors to come and rejoice with her. "I had lost one of my drachmas," she says, "and I have found it." Five of her women friends come running to the lamp-lit room. The widow brings out some dried fruit and cake. Her friends laugh and rejoice with her; they understand how serious her loss has been and how happy she is.

Again, Jesus left no doubt as to the meaning of this simple

human story. The Holy One of Israel, he told the crowd, rejoices over every lost person just as this woman rejoices in finding her coin. Yahweh, Abba, cares about every human being just as this woman cares about the coin she lost. Every lost person is of inestimable value to the divine Lover.

The Lost Son

These two parables lead up to the great parable that is sometimes called the gospel within the gospel. They set the stage for a picture of the unconditional love that Abba has for human beings. No tale of the master story-teller expresses more fully the essence of Jesus' understanding of the nature of heaven, Abba, the divine Holy One — or of Jesus' own ministry — than this incisive account of the substantial Hebrew landholder with two sons. Popularly known as the Parable of the Prodigal Son, this story speaks more centrally about the extravagant love of a prodigal father than of the son's escapades. The story provides us with a guide to Jesus' intimate knowledge of the divine Creator. This story reveals clearly the radical, revolutionary nature of Jesus' mission and message.

Try to imagine yourself one of the mixed crowd of Jews listening to Jesus, as he told about the prosperous farmer and how he deals with his two sons. If this story appears absurd to us, it would have seemed even more preposterous to those who first heard it. The younger son is about seventeen when he makes his startling request. He has traveled to the cities of Tiberias and Sepphoris, and he knows the comforts and excitement of these Roman cities with a Greek population. He says to himself: "Life is really dull here on the ranch, and I want to live, live, live. At home everyone is working and having little real fun. Soon the best years of my life will be gone. I will go and ask for my inheritance and my freedom." He gathers up his courage, makes up his little speech, and then goes to his father, who is resting after a hard day. Without introduction he bursts out: "Father, I do not think that I am cut out for life as a farmer, and life here is monotonous. I want to make my own way in the real world. Give me my inheritance now and let me go." Few modern parents would be completely surprised with such a request, but it was unthinkable for a child to speak this way to a parent in the Jewish society of Jesus' time. Children simply did not speak to their fathers that way. In addition, the son's request implies (not too subtly) that he wishes his father were dead.

Jesus' listeners were aghast. With this beginning Jesus caught their total attention. They were even more astounded when Jesus went on to tell the father's response. The father, Abba, listens quietly, embraces his son warmly, and says: "You can have your share in seven days. We will make an accounting for you." Meanwhile the servants on the other side of a thin partition hear every word and stare at one another in disbelief. What could have happened to their master? And when the older brother meets one of the servants bubbling over with the news, he secretly wonders if his father has lost his wits; he wanders off into the hills to collect himself before coming home.

Soon everyone in the small Galilean village knows that the younger son is about to turn his property into gold and go off to a big city. When he comes to the village to turn his inheritance into cash, the merchants are ready for him. They offer him hardly half what his goods and chattel are worth, but the boy is seventeen and impatient, and takes what he can get. He says his goodbyes, gets into the saddle of his new horse, and rides off on a Roman road. The absurdity of this story is so great that many of the listeners must have laughed out loud at the stupidity of the father and his son; it is worth noting the humor in Jesus' stories, the comic relief, which too often we fail to observe.

The young man sets out for Antioch. In the Roman cities nearby, he has learned of this city where everything is possible. Obviously no city in Jewish territory would be wild enough for him, but Antioch is known as the most decadent city of the morally decadent Roman world. As he journeys, he stays at the best inns and finally comes to his destination.

And where does our newly rich young man first go when he

reaches Antioch? Undoubtedly he seeks out the Roman bath, where he finds scores of young men and women just like him. They tell him where the best apartments are to be found, and he settles into one. (Decency forbids that I describe in any detail what went on in a Roman bath. Suffice it to say that it was a pornographic bookstore in 3-D.) The young man from the country has a generous supply of gold, solid currency in that age as well as in our own; with it he begins his riotous and reckless living, filled with wine, women and song.

The time passes quickly. Some six months later he realizes suddenly that his cache of gold coins is low and then gone. Those who have shared the grasshopper summer with him laugh at his entreaties for help and will have nothing more to do with him. At the very same time, one of the frequent famines strikes the land. Our brash young man has no skill but enthusiasm, and he can find no work. One by one he sells all the treasurers he has acquired. When these are gone, he does not even have any money for food. He grows hungrier and hungrier. At last, in order to survive, he hires out to a wealthy landowner to feed and tend his pigs.

Again, to appreciate the full significance of this detail, we need to place ourselves in the position of the Jews who were listening. The youth had already broken the moral law of the Torah by his riotous living, but Jewish religious tradition was remarkably realistic about human weakness in sexual matters, and in the Jewish economy of scarcity, overindulgence was, ironically, judged quite leniently. The book of Proverbs warns against prostitutes, but on the other hand prostitutes were common, and at least one prostitute, Rahab, was a national heroine. Jesus' listeners would have agreed that this young man was certainly off base and very foolish, but they would have felt that his hedonism was natural and normal.

But feeding and tending pigs was quite another matter; this was a flagrant violation of the ritual law. It was forbidden in the Torah to eat pork, to touch the carcass of a pig, or to offer swine's blood in sacrifice (cf. Lev 11:7-8; Dt 14:8; Is 65:4). In the Talmud, a later elaboration of the Jewish law, the pig was the very symbol of ritual uncleanness, and those who tended pigs were treated with aversion bordering on disgust. This attitude would have been shared by all those to whom Jesus spoke. A gasp of horror rose from the crowd as Jesus shared the utter degradation of the younger son. Those who touched a pig were unclean four times as long as those who visited a prostitute; the prodigal has not only broken the moral law but has totally defiled himself, as much as if he had bathed in a cesspool. The only comparable horror with which I can compare his act is the attitude toward fornication and adultery found in Boston and the puritan colonies in 1700.

At last the broken youth comes to his senses, not because of a great moral conversion but because of a pinched stomach. When he comes to himself, he does not consider his father's love and mercy and goodness and return for these. He only wants to fill his stomach; he thinks to himself that even his father's servants and slaves have more than enough to eat. He is starving and longing to eat the very food that he feeds to the pigs. He is utterly disgusted with the defiling task that he is doing. He reasons with himself: "It is better to live than to die in this awful place. I will set out for home, and I will only ask to be a lowly servant or even a slave." He works out what he will tell his father and comes up with these words: "Father, I have sinned against heaven and before you; I am no longer worthy to be called your son; treat me as one of your hired hands." Almost immediately he starts on his homeward trek.

The Prodigal Returns

The prodigal has made no attempt to contact his family for the many months that he has been gone. And when his father receives no news of his son, the father's heart grows heavier and heavier. He does not know whether his son is alive or dead, and not knowing can be as difficult for the human heart as hearing the worst news. Every day in the cool of the morning, the father goes out to a hill, the highest point on his property; he searches the horizon in every direction, hoping to see some sign of his returning son. Again at sunset, he goes out to scan the whole countryside.

One day, after many months, he sees a dark speck on a far-off hillside; it is a human figure. Even at that distance, the father knows it is his lost child; he recognizes his much-loved son with the clear-sightedness that — as Laurens Van der Post says — loving people always have:

> If there is one thing that love is not, it is blind. If it possesses a blindness at all, it is a blindness to the man and the man-made blindnesses of life; to the dead-ends, the cul-de-sacs and hopelessnesses of our being. In all else it is clear and far-sighted as the sun. When the world and judgment say: "This is the end," love alone can see the way out. It is the aboriginal tracker, the African bushman on the faded desert spoor within us, and its unfailing quarry is always the light.[4]

To appreciate the meeting of the father and son, one needs to understand both the Greek words used to describe the father's actions and also Semitic custom at that time. First of all, the father *races* toward his son as soon as he recognizes him: The Greek word is the same one used to describe running a foot race in Greek athletic games. A Semitic man of the father's age walked with dignity, and the father would not have raced anywhere in many years. In order to run he must either tuck his long robe into his girdle or take it in his hand — and then (shamefully) his underwear might show.

When the father starts to run, his servants and any other villagers around know that something of immense importance is about to take place. When the father reaches his son, he flings his arms around him and holds him to his bosom, kissing him again and again with compassionate care.[5] The son hardly knows what is happening as he is gathered into the father's arms. He begins to stammer out his well-prepared little speech, but he never has a chance to finish it. His father cuts him off and begins to give orders to his servants, who have followed and are standing awestruck behind him.

The servants return as quickly as possible bearing three gifts of incredible significance: a robe, a ring and a pair of shoes. Although a tradition of long standing among biblical critics has stated dogmatically that parables can only have one central meaning, and most commentators follow this tradition without thinking, I propose that the added detail of these gifts supplements the parable's meaning in a deeply symbolic way. In *Transforming Bible Study*, Walter Wink has pointed out clearly that each part of a parable can be a symbol of unfathomable meaning, just as each image in a dream can lead deep into mystery. One of the reasons Jesus speaks to the depth of the human heart as much today as ever is that he not only engages our rational thinking mind, but he also speaks in the universal language of symbols. The universal symbolic language used by Jesus is the same language that the soul speaks in dreams.[6]

Nearly every great modern artist who has tried visually to represent the story of the Prodigal Son has depicted the son with his head buried in his father's bosom. Instead of dispatching the son to go home and shower and shave, the father tells his servant to bring the son the *best* robe; the father then places the robe around the shoulders of his son, who is still filthy from the swine swill mixed with the dirt of the road. Why does Abba act this way toward his son? The father has already made plans for a great feast, at which he will invite all the family friends to rejoice with him, because his son was dead and is alive again, was lost and is found. It is not easy to be a prodigal returning home and being greeted by so many guests. The old family friends will come and ask: "And where have you been?" But by giving his son a fine robe, the father is trying to stave off as much of this embarrassment as possible. An ordinary new robe would not have demonstrated his unconditional love for his son. This family robe signifies that the father and his guests are honored to have the lost son return; he is the revered guest.

The Robe, the Ring and the Shoes

In addition, the detail of the robe gives me the impression of a certain impatience in the father. He wants the son's image restored immediately so that the son might begin to change his own self-image. Clothes are very important. In the modern business world, they are one key to business success and social acceptance; in dreams they represent the face we show to the world — our "persona," as Jung calls it. (Remember that Jesus told another story about a person who comes to a wedding feast without the proper wedding garment; this signifies that the man is unprepared, without the right attitude.) So the father knows that his son's dismal self-image has to change before the son will be able to allow himself to be received. The new image is given by the father as pure, free gift. Imagine how relieved the son must be when he strips off his old, torn, foul-smelling dirty clothes. The gift of the robe, then, is an act of compassion in many different ways and on many different levels.

The father asks the servants to hand him the ruby signet ring set in gold, and he places it upon his son's grimy hand. The youth needs the shoes and the robe, but isn't the gift of a ring overdoing it a bit? Why *that* ring? The Greek is very clear: Such a ring is far more than an ornament, although it is that too. This ring gives the returned wastrel legal authority in the family. The father gives his son the kind of ring that, in Hebrew society, was used to sign a contract or a will. Even today such a ring is used by villagers in the Near East to sign official documents. In China and Japan, a painting or document is still signed with a "chop," an engraved ring or seal bearing the name of the owner. So even though the son has wasted his share of the family fortune, he is now legally integrated back into the family estate. (No wonder the older brother is furious.) In addition, a ring is a deep traditional symbol of relationship: For many centuries rings have been used as symbols of the union of marriage. The gift of the ring, then, signifies the father's incredible forgiveness of his son. How utterly unjust this is, from one point of view! Jesus' story, however, is not about justice, but about something greater than justice — full-throated, unbounded, gracious mercy and unconditional love.

And then there is the gift of the shoes. The son needs the shoes. His feet are torn and bleeding. His own shoes long ago were worn out and fell apart. The young man has traveled the long distance home over rough roads in bare feet. Slaves and bond-servants did not wear shoes in the ancient world; their feet developed thick calluses, rough and hard. But the prodigal is the son of a householder and has been brought up in shoes, so his feet have not been hardened. The gift of shoes snatches him right out of the class of servant and makes him a son again. This gift, therefore, signifies mercy on several levels. In addition, shoes are a recurrent dream symbol signifying our standpoint, our basic stance, our view of reality. Symbolically, then, a new view of himself and of those around him has been given to the son. Seldom do we achieve this new vision by ourselves; it is *given*. So it is with amazed gratitude that the son places the shoes upon his feet.

Slowly father and son, along with servants and a growing crowd, wind their way back toward the father's house. The father orders the fatted calf to be slaughtered and prepares for a great feast. Any kind of meat is a delicacy in that world, but this is the choicest prime meat. (Once, when a class of children was studying this story, the teacher asked them, "Whom do you feel most sorry for?" One little girl spoke up with a sob in her voice: "The fatted calf.")

The Banquet and the Elder Brother

Preparations are made for a great party, one like the wedding that Jesus attended in Cana. The calf is roasted, and every servant helps in preparing the sumptuous banquet. Musicians are summoned to provide music. All the invited guests attend the party, since they know the generosity of their host. The prodigal had returned in the morning, and by evening a gala crowd gathers to welcome back the lost son. There is joyous music and dancing, and the best wine flows freely.

In the meantime the older son returns from his day in the
fields. It has been a long, hot, hard day; the sun has begun to set,
and the older son is tired. As he approaches the central house of
the estate, he hears music and sees the flicker of many torches.
When he left in the morning, he had heard no mention of regal
festivities that same night, so he wonders what his strange father
is up to now. At that moment he sees a slave boy, who is
obviously elated. He calls the boy over to him and asks what is
going on. The boy is happy about the party, because all the slaves
and servants will share in what is left over. The slave blurts out:
"Your brother has come home, and your father has killed the
fatted calf because he has received him back safe and sound. He
has invited all the neighbors, and has thrown the biggest feast I
have ever seen." The slave boy is happy, because the younger son
has always been kind to him even though he is a slave.

At this the older brother is enraged. He cuffs the slave boy.
Then he orders the boy back to the party to tell his father, "Your
older son is angry and won't come to your stupid feast." Like
many who see themselves as righteous, the older brother is
unable to feel mercy or compassion. After all, his brother already
received his share of the property. This magnificent party is
coming out of the older son's inheritance.

The refusal of this older son to come to the party would in
many ways have seemed to Jesus' listeners a far greater breach
of Semitic morality, manners and etiquette than the wildness of
the prodigal. This is defiance and rejection of the father and his
values. The prodigal has been a fool and has returned home, and
even in Hebrew society, it would have been possible for the
audience to imagine him being grafted back onto the family
(though perhaps not with the lavish extravagance described in
the story). The older brother, however, has utterly defied his
father, rejected him. In a way he is calling his father a fool. He is
totally defiant; he breaks the fourth commandment of Moses: to
honor one's parents. He may continue to do his work, but he is
severing any real relation with his father.

Far more extravagant than the son's anger is the father's

response to his older son. The idea of forgiveness has not been central to the cultures of the Middle East. It was unthinkable to most of Jesus' listeners that the host father would quietly leave the party and go out to his insolent son. Nonetheless, he does just that, and when he tries to reach out to his son and plead with him, the older brother's vitriol pours out upon his parent. Going out to his arrogant son is in many ways a greater act of forgiveness and mercy, more of breaking of customary mores than the reception of his wayward son. This father not only goes the second mile, he goes seven times seventy miles.

Jesus minced no words in describing the older son's angry, vitriolic response to his father: "Listen!" the son says. "For all these years I have been working like a slave for you, and I have never disobeyed your command; yet you have never given me even a young goat so that I might celebrate with my friends. But when this son of yours came back, who has devoured your property with prostitutes, you killed the fatted calf for him." Jesus' audience undoubtedly expected an equally angry response from the father. Instead the father speaks with love, reconciliation, forgiveness to his impudent son: "Son, you are always with me, and all that is mine is yours. But we had to celebrate and rejoice because your brother was dead and has come to life; he was lost and has been found." Jesus has expressed to his listeners his realization that the Holy One of Israel is like this father. The Holy One is so secure in the power of love and forgiveness that defiance does not change Abba's outgoing love. Not only does Abba receive young fools who have gone astray, but Abba also goes out to stiff, workaholic, self-righteous scribes and Pharisees.

The Incredible Love of God

So often we forget the second part of the story and fail to realize that the parable's full message is that *God loves us all*. Abba would prefer us to be honest in dealing with the holy than to put on pious masks and to be afraid to express our frustration, pain and rage; even the older son's stiff, self-righteous defiance is forgivable. Abba is the only one to whom we can express our failures and our rage and cause no damage. So it is important that we acknowledge even our folly or stuffiness; then we can come and enjoy the banquet of the reign of heaven with our eternal Abba.

Many years ago I was lecturing at an ecumenical retreat center in Germany. We were gathered together for the final presentation. Many of the participants brought along their musical instruments; an orchestra of forty people had been organized. As the music began, a group that had been studying the importance of symbols acted out the entire story of the prodigal in pantomime. Then, as all the people in the story gathered together for the banquet, the great doors of Schloss Craheim were flung open and tables laden with bread and wine and fruit were carried in, and we celebrated eucharist. We were all invited to the feast of the younger and the older brother; both had returned home to the father's joy. I realized in a new way that the eucharist is the celebration of *all* of us wandering prodigals and self-righteous judges, coming home to Abba. This service is the feast of all younger brothers and sisters and older brothers and sisters who have turned around and come home to Abba's fellowship and company. This is why the early Church called the liturgy a love feast, an agape.

Jesus was a master story-teller, and so his story breaks off with the father and son talking together. What happens to these characters? I believe that the older brother finally softens and comes reluctantly back to his father's feast. He eats and drinks and talks to his friends. Suddenly he realizes that he can have not only a young goat for a feast with his friends, but even a fatted calf whenever he wants one. He has not allowed himself to see his father's bounty. Over the succeeding weeks and months and years, he allows the love and mercy and kindness of the father to penetrate his heart. He and his brother become friends.

A deeply religious woman came into my office in the church I served. She and her husband had been missionaries in the Philippines. They both took their religion and spiritual lives very seriously. She had come to see me before about growing spiritually. On this visit she began to weep as she sat down. She was hurt and angry. Her husband of over thirty years was having an affair with another woman; now he had left home and was living with that other woman. Letty felt betrayed by her husband and her God. She was furious. I listened as she poured out her tale of woe, knowing that she needed to express her feelings to someone. I did no more than listen to her with openness and sympathy.

Two weeks later Letty came to see me again. Her attitude was entirely different. She had been meditating on the story of the two sons. She realized that she had been playing the part of the older brother in the story and that she needed to learn to forgive and to love. She now felt in no position to judge her husband. She asked me to pray with and for her. We went into the church and prayed that the Holy Spirit would change her attitude and that of her husband as well. Without any contact between them, her husband returned home later that week. They forgave each other and lived together another fifteen years, and her husband took loving care of her in her terminal illness. Miracles do happen. Jung once said to me: "When your soul is ready to receive other people, the souls of others will know, and they will come and ask you to be with them in their need."

The Dishonest Manager

Jesus followed his story of the Prodigal Son with still another story of forgiveness, which he delivered to the hushed crowd before him. It is a strange story and hard for our materialistic society to understand. In this story a manager of a large estate finds that he is about to be fired for inefficiency. Still in charge of accounts, he settles huge accounts with his master's debtors to the debtors' benefit. He knows that this will guarantee that he will have places where he will be welcome after he is fired; these debtors will be indebted to him. Instead of rebuking the manager, Jesus praised him for acting shrewdly. He then lamented sadly that those dealing with business matters put more effort into worldly things than the religious (the children of light) put into knowing and loving the Holy One and one another. Our growth in loving, Jesus was saying, ought to be a far greater priority than seeking to succeed in the outer world; actions of love have eternal consequences.

Jesus' parables are great, powerful stories. And yet, I doubt if I could take the stories Jesus told very seriously if I did not know the story that he lived. Again and again I think of two statues in the great basilica in the center of the University of Notre Dame. On one side of the high altar in this church is a magnificent bronze statue by Ivan Mestrovic of the prodigal returned, with his head buried in his father's arms. On the other side of the altar is a monumental marble of the Pieta by the same sculptor, with Joseph of Arimathea standing behind Mary, who is holding the body of her son. One is the story Jesus told, the other the story that he lived.

The Holy One of Israel, Abba, created our universe in its infinite complexity, then came into the world as a baby in a manger in Bethlehem on our planet earth, and then became a political refugee in Egypt. Jesus suffered with us, suffered on the cross for us, rose again triumphantly from the dead, and threw open the portals of the fellowship of heaven for us. The story of the prodigal and the history of the cross and resurrection tell the same story of Abba's incredible, unconditional love for all of us lost and hurting human beings — and for dutiful older brothers as well.

The Greatest Gift in the World

Few words in the English language are more ambiguous than the word "love." I had realized that the word needs to be described carefully, for I knew that "love" has many different meanings: zero in scoring tennis; mere sexual passion; the deepest kind of mutual, life-long caring between two people; a name for the Divine; the highest form of mystical encounter or union with the Holy. However, only as I began to meditate on Jesus' stories and life and upon the meaning of the word *love* in the Old and New Testaments did I discover that "love" is found five hundred times in the Bible. To make things even more complicated, our one English word "love" translates thirteen different Hebrew words and fifteen different Greek words, and my unabridged *Webster's Dictionary* tells me that in English the word "love" has *at least seventy different* meanings. So if we are to practice the art of Christian love, we need to be very clear about the nature of that "love"; it is the divine essence and also our guide to encounter the holy or the risen Christ and to relate to one another.[1]

Few people deny the value of human love. Indeed, we find love praised in nearly all great literature, as well as in the Bible and in thousands of Christian hymns. The centrality of love is found in all the major religions and in all profound spiritual practice.[2] Whenever human beings search for the ultimate meaning in life, they begin to talk about "love." As I studied the letters of Paul, I discovered that the words "love" and "Holy Spirit" could be interchanged without altering his meaning. And modern writers agree with Paul. At the age of ninety-two, after spending his whole life writing about human history, Will Durant stated that the final lesson of history could be summed up in three words: *love one another*. He went on to say that he

41

embraced Jesus' teaching of the centrality of love and that he considered love the most practical thing in the world. Many years ago, furthermore, a counselee drew my attention to a passage at the conclusion of Jung's autobiography, *Memories, Dreams, Reflections*. I had missed its deep significance when I had read the book. Jung states that the essence of love is hidden in the mystery of God, and that the two experiences cannot be separated. He goes on to say that the mystery of love might as well be described as the mystery of God.

Richard Coan, a student of human wholeness and maturity, writes that saintliness is one essential ingredient of the actualized life. He describes saints as those who reach out to others with compassion, caring and empathy, using the same kind of devotion they have experienced in their encounter with the divine. He quotes the novelist James Baldwin: "The moment we cease to hold each other, the moment we break faith with one another, the sea engulfs us and the light goes out."[3]

Aldous Huxley looks at the way the word "love" is profaned and concludes:

> Of all the worn, smudged, dog-eared words in our vocabulary, "love" is surely the grubbiest, smelliest, slimiest. Bawled from a million pulpits, lasciviously crooned through hundreds of millions of loud speakers, it has become an outrage to good taste and decent feeling, an obscenity which one hesitates to pronounce. And yet it has to be pronounced, for, after all, *Love* is the last word.[4]

In his book, *Love, Medicine, and Miracles*, Bernie Siegel, a cancer surgeon, tells of his work with his patients. He writes that healing involves psychology and spirituality, as well as surgery. He states again and again that a loving environment and the patient's capacity to love are the determining factors in *all* cures that defy statistics. Most psychological and religious healers similarly emphasize the vital importance of love as the catalyst in healing.

In his recent book *Healing Words*, Larry Dossey, M.D., not only relates his own experiences of the healing power of love and prayer, but also gives a comprehensive survey of the experimental evidence that love heals and that loving prayer heals. He points out how love actually changes our bodies with blushing, palpitations and other physiological changes. (Other emotions also affect our bodies. We are sad and we cry, and there is a healing agent in the tears.) People will rally from near death for their beloved. Dossey concludes his discussion of love and healing with these words: "Love occupies a majestic place in healing. Lying outside of space and time it is a living tissue of reality, a bond that unites us all."[5]

What Is Love?

Before I write another word, let me express clearly and bluntly that I am a beginner in understanding the nature of human and divine love. I have been meditating on the subject nearly daily for thirty years (since my enlightenment on the plane which I described earlier). I am also a beginner in the practice of embodying Christian love; when I try to speak lovingly, I often say too little or too much. We are dealing with a mystery, the mystery that lies in the essence of the divine Creator — the mystery the Holy One has woven into the very fabric of our universe, culminating in our bodies, minds and souls. We have already seen that human life and consciousness usually wither and die without love. If we deny the reality of both divine and human love, we are not dealing honestly with the universe in which we live — we are blind to the core of reality. As we try to describe love, we will not be able to explain exactly what love is, but we will understand more about its nature and unfathomable depth. Such hypothetical self-correcting understanding reflects the way humans gain knowledge. For instance, we grow in knowledge of the physical world, as we try to explain what we know; we then discover that some detail does not fit our explanation, and we try to find a better explanation. We grow in our knowledge of the spiritual dimension of reality and love in the same way.

My friend John Sanford and I have talked again and again about the mysterious nature of love. I will never forget his statement to me: "I know a good bit about sexuality. I know a good bit about transference (the loving concern so necessary if successful psychological counseling is to be helpful). And I know something about love. However, when I add all this together, I know absolutely nothing." It is only with some fear and trepidation that I undertake to write on the subject of love, divine and human, but in spite of my inadequacy and limited understanding, I agree with Aldous Huxley that love is the last word. I would be more remiss *not* to try to describe what I have learned from the Bible and Church history, and what I have experienced myself, than to do so in an inadequate manner. You will notice that I have used the word "describe," not the word "define." We can *define* only a logical idea. In fact, even mathematics is mysterious, and the physics of quantum mechanics cannot be explained to human satisfaction.[6] When we talk about "love," we are dealing with a living reality that will be expressed in a slightly different way by each human being — just as no two leaves are exactly the same and no two fingerprints are identical. And yet we can make many true statements about the nature of love culled from the history of spirituality. We can give clear examples of love in action, and we can state how different it is from its imitations.

When we begin to describe love, we are trying to understand the ultimate nature of reality, the divine Lover who created the world so that we human beings might enjoy the very Reality that created us. We are also talking about the God-given capacity implanted in us, the ability to enable us to receive and to give love. Augustine writes that we were made restless in order that we might seek and find our full meaning in our growing relationship to the Holy One; this meaning is beyond space and time. In four inspired lines of poetry, Emily Dickinson describes the essence of this reality:

Love — is anterior to Life —
Posterior — to Death —
Initial of Creation, and
The exponent of Earth.[7]

The great theologian and student of mysticism, Baron von Hügel, wrote that the only way to study mysticism is to study the lives of mystics. Likewise the only way to understand the incredible reality of divine love is to listen to those who have had direct encounters with divine love. Perhaps the finest modern account of such a revelation of the risen Jesus and of the divine Love is written by the profound religious writer and fine theologian, Henri Nouwen. Nouwen confirmed my conviction that only as human love is patterned after and energized by divine love can it become the greatest gift in the world.

Nouwen's Experience of Divine Love

A few years ago the middle-aged Nouwen was struck down by the rear vision mirror of a large truck and thrown down to the icy side of the road. He was taken to the hospital, where he grew weaker. He realized that his life was ebbing away. For the first time in his life, he decided to look seriously at the possibility that he was dying. He tried to let go of his familiar world and looked for a door that might open to him. He wrote the following words, as he reflected on the vision that unexpectedly opened before him. I quote his words at length; any summary of them would inadequately convey the depth of his profound experience:

> When I entered the portal of death, I experienced what I had never experienced before: pure and unconditional love. No, that is not the best way to express it. What I encountered was an intensely personal presence that pushed all my fears aside. It was a very gentle, nonjudging presence, a presence that simply asked me to trust completely.
> I hesitate to speak simply about Jesus, because that name might not evoke the full divine presence that I experienced.

My whole life up to that point had been an arduous attempt to follow Jesus as I had come to know him through my parents, friends, and teachers. I had spent countless hours studying scripture, listening to lectures and sermons, and reading spiritual books. Jesus had been very close to me but also very distant, a friend but also a stranger, a source of hope but also a fear, guilt, and shame. Now, as I walked around the portal of death, all ambiguity and all uncertainty were gone. He was there, the Lord of my life, saying, "Come, don't be afraid. I love you." His presence was deeply human as well as deeply divine, very personal but so much greater than my imaginings. I knew without doubt that he was there for me, but also that he was embracing the universe. I knew he was the Jesus I had prayed to and spoken about, but also that now he did not ask for prayers or words. All was well.

The words that summarize it all are *life* and *love*. But these words were incarnate in a real presence. Death lost its power and shrank before the Life and Love that surrounded me in such an intimate way.

One emotion was very strong — that of homecoming. Jesus opened his home to me and seemed to say, "Here is where you belong." The words he spoke to his disciples became very real:

"There are many rooms in my Father's house. . . . I am going now to prepare a place for you" (John 14:2, JB). The risen Jesus, who now dwells with his Father, was welcoming me home after a long journey. My homecoming had a real quality of return, a return to the womb of God. The God who had fashioned me in secret and molded me in the depths of the earth, the God who had knitted me together in my mother's womb, was calling me back and *wanted to receive me as someone who had become child enough to be loved as a child.*[8]

Nouwen's statement that he "had become child enough to be loved as a child" has a powerful emotional resonance. It is easy for most of us to love small children most of the time. They usually respond to love and caring, if they are well and have not been abused. In addition, children need unconditional love: to love children only when they are good is using them, not loving them. Children learn love as they are loved. Most of what they do that causes us frustration and anger is due to our impatience and ignorance or lack of understanding of the nature of the growing child. When we realize this truth, it is much easier to maintain a loving atmosphere.

And Nouwen's description of his retrieval of his own childhood harmonizes with the words of Jesus. A group of women came up to Jesus asking him to bless their children. The disciples did not realize the depth of children's needs and the wisdom and inclusiveness of Jesus' love: They actually tried to shoo the children away. Jesus then turned to his disciples and spoke to them brusquely: "Let the little children come to me, and do not stop them; for it is to such as these that the kingdom of God belongs. Truly I tell you. Whoever does not receive the kingdom of God as a little child will never enter it" (Lk 18:16-17; cf. Mk 10:13-15; Mt 19:13-15).

As Nouwen felt himself weakening, he had the deep desire to forgive and to be forgiven. He had left Yale Divinity School to minister at Daybreak, a home for disadvantaged children. He told a friend from Daybreak: "Please tell everyone who has hurt me that I forgive them from my heart, and please ask everyone whom I have hurt to forgive me too."[9] Nouwen realized that forgiveness is an essential element of the community of heaven, of the Holy One and of mature human relationships.

In my first parish, one lonely person became quite attached to the church and to me. The community was a poor one, and she helped make the church grow and make it financially solvent. When I moved to the west coast, she came to see my new church and my family several times. Gradually, however, the relationship died, largely because I let it die. But the night before an operation during which she died, she sent me a card. On it she wrote that she forgave me for my allowing my concern for her to dissolve. I remember the sense of gratitude and the relief that her last letter gave me. Lela had learned true Christian love. I only wish that I had kept that note.

In one of his finest books, *The Great Divorce*, C. S. Lewis tells the story of a group of people in hell who are given a vacation in heaven. One of them is an ordinary, decent man who has never cheated on his wife, has paid his bills, and has never been in legal trouble. The first person that this visitor meets in heaven is a man whom he had known well on earth — a man who had been convicted and hanged for committing murder. Enraged, the newcomer blurts out: "How did you ever get in here?" Speaking in a soft and kindly voice, the murderer replies: "By the bloody mercy of Jesus Christ." The visitor growls back: "I don't want anyone's bloody mercy." Then he turns his back on heaven and enters the next bus bound for hell. Forgiveness and mercy had no place in his morality. Lewis' point is that one can by one's own volition shut out the unconditional divine love; heaven is never forced upon us.

As Nouwen slowly regained his strength and recovered, he reflected upon his experience of the unconditional mercy and love of the Beloved. He came to two new insights. To fulfill his ministry, he needed to proclaim the reality of Christ's love in a new way. He also realized that the way we die can be a culmination of our living and can deeply affect the lives of those around us. Nouwen wrote:

> I believe that I am asked to proclaim the love of God in a new way. Until now, I have been thinking and speaking from time to eternity, from a passing reality to a lasting reality, from the experience of human love to the love of God. But after touching "the other side," it seems that a new proclamation is needed — a proclamation that speaks back into the world of ambiguities from the place of unconditional love. This is such a radical change that I may find it hard, even impossible, to discover the words that can reach

the hearts of my fellow human beings. But I sense that words must emerge and awaken the deepest longing of the human heart.[10]

I know of no better statement of the goal of the followers of Christ than this: proclaiming to this world of ambiguities the reality of the love at the heart and center of the universe. We share this love not only by words, but also by the way we live in the world and interact with one another and by the way we die.

When my thirty-four-year-old son John died six years ago, I learned the truth of Nouwen's second insight: "We have a choice: We can bind with guilt and fear or set free with gratitude." Before I read *Beyond the Mirror*, the book in which Nouwen describes his near-death experience, I had not realized why there had been a holy quality in the four months my wife and I cared for John in his apartment by the sea. We tried to provide for his needs as he experienced them. We talked in depth and forgave one another. We spent whatever time he wanted with us, night and day.

John looked forward to a new adventure. He shared with us his hope of new life, and he released us from all guilt. When I read these words of Nouwen, I found them deeply familiar and true: "In this perspective life is a long journey of preparation, of preparing oneself to truly die for others. It is a series of little deaths in which we are asked to move increasingly from clinging to others to living for them."[11] Nouwen opened my eyes to another facet of the jewel of love that I had seen twice, as I meditated in the silence on two different long plane trips. I realized how much John had truly lived for us during those last four months.

Experiences of this kind are not limited to theologians and professional ministers. They occur everywhere. In thirty years of lecturing all over the world, I have discovered that people will tell of their numinous experiences of the holy and their intimations of divine homecoming if they know that we have a place in our world view for these realities and will not ridicule them. I have collected hundreds of these experiences; I have also recently written an introduction to G. Scott Sparrow's book *Lo, I Am with You Always*, in which Sparrow describes dozens of experiences of people who have had visions of Christ.

Two Other Experiences of Heaven

Before Nouwen wrote of his experience, a woman from Texas told me a similar experience and then wrote it down for me. During a dinner with friends at a restaurant, the woman suffered a massive stroke. She was rushed to the hospital and was treated. She was not expected to live. She wondered what it would be like to die. Her condition stabilized, and she went to sleep; later she wrote down what she experienced:

> Then I had a dream that changed my life. I dreamed that I was in a wonderful place. There was great peace and joy. I realized that I would not be put down by anyone — it was a place of pure love, and love was the center of everyone there. I was so happy that everyone there loved everyone, and there would be no anger there.
>
> There were angels flying around, and our priest was there. There were others there, but attention was focused on the priest and angels. I realized that the important thing in my life was to love everybody, and then we all would be in accord.
>
> It was the most beautiful dream I have ever had, and the feeling that was there was pure unadulterated love and such joy to know that this was what heaven would be like.
>
> Then my recovery came rapidly. Everyone was amazed (me included)! Then there came thoughts into my life of things I had done and said in the past that I certainly was not proud of. It seemed to me that I had become inflated over the glorious dream and thought I had it made into heaven. Now I am busy repenting of the things that came up out of my past and making amends where I can and also

being very happy loving everyone. I hope that I can continue in this way of living because everyday seems good. I have no fear of death. I love God, Father, Son and Holy Spirit and my husband Joe and my family and others. I pray for joy on this earth and forever.[12]

The Holy One is always searching out lost sheep and lost sons and daughters. Thomas Wolfe did not even know that he was sick when he wrote the final lines of his last novel, *You Can't Go Home Again*. Nothing else in Wolfe's writing is like this passage; his words are particularly significant because they emerge from one who had little connection with organized religion. It is one of the finest expressions of the Christian vision of the home the Holy One prepares for us. Wolfe had experienced a vision of the night that had touched the deepest level of eternal reality:

Dear Fox, old friend, thus we have come to the end of the road that we were to go together . . . and so farewell.

But before I go, I have just one more thing to tell you:

Something has spoken to me in the night, burning the tapers of the waning year; something has spoken in the night, and told me I shall die, I know not where. Saying:

"To lose the earth you know, for greater knowing; to lose the life you have, for greater life; to leave the friends you loved, for greater loving; to find a land more kind than home, more large than earth —

— Whereon the pillars of this earth are founded, toward which the conscience of the world is tending — a wind is rising, and the rivers flow."[13]

Wolfe's last written words were a note to Maxwell Perkins, the editor who had discovered the author and established him as one of the leading novelists of his time. They had become estranged, and Wolfe did not want to die unforgiven or unforgiving. His vision of the night had touched the depth of him.

Dear Max:

I'm sneaking this against orders, but I've got a hunch — and I wanted to write these words to you.

I've made a long voyage and been to a strange country, and I've seen the dark man very close; I don't think I was too much afraid of him, but so much of mortality still clings to me — I wanted most desperately to live and still do . . . and there was the impossible anguish and regret of all the work I had not done, of all the work I had to do. . . .

Whatever happens — I had this "hunch" and wanted to write you and tell you, no matter what happens or has happened, I shall always think of you and feel about you the way it was that Fourth of July day three years ago when you met me at the boat and we went out on the cafe on the river . . . and later went on top of the tall building, and all the strangeness and the glory and the power of life and of the city was below.

Yours always, Tom.

Wolfe was making ready for *greater knowing*, greater life, greater loving, a land more kind than home, more large than earth.

When human beings are deeply moved, they often begin to sing and dance and write poetry, so it is not surprising that much great art deals with the encounter with the Holy One. No experience of human love compares with the utter joy of knowing that we are loved by the Holy One now and always. There is nothing left to fear. All will be well. All will be well. These sentiments are expressed in nearly every hymn we sing; such songs of joy and hope are an integral part of Christian worship. I asked a very capable Chinese woman, an accountant in Singapore, what had drawn her to Christianity from her non-Christian background. She replied without hesitation: "As a child I passed by a Christian school and heard the joyous, happy songs they were singing. My religion did not provide this kind of joy. I found what I was looking for." Against angry opposition from her family she made the change once she was an adult and had moved away from home.

One of the most magnificent pieces of Christian poetry was written by John of the Cross. He had been working to bring vitality and life back into his religious order. The authorities of his order felt that he was being disruptive, and they put him in the monastery jail and fed him on bread and water in order to bring him to his senses. There he did indeed come to his senses, and he had a religious experience that he expressed in one of the finest examples of Spanish poetry. This poem provided the base for all his future writing. After the experience expressed in this poetry, John escaped from his dungeon and founded a new order of Carmelites. John's poem's depth and tenderness of feeling reveal an utter honesty and emotional tenderness that few in the secular world dare express.

Stanzas of the Soul

1. On a dark night, Kindled in love with yearnings
      — oh, happy chance! —
   I went forth without being observed, My house being now
         at rest.
2. In darkness and secure, By the secret ladder, disguised
      — oh, happy chance! —
   In darkness and in concealment, My house being now at rest.
3. In the happy night, In secret, when none saw me,
   Nor I beheld aught, without light or guide, save that
         which burned in my heart.
4. This light guided me More surely than the light of noonday,
   To the place where he (well I knew who!) was awaiting me
      — A place where none appeared.
5. Oh, night that guided me, Oh, night more lovely than
         the dawn,
   Oh, night that joined Beloved with lover, Love transformed
      in the Beloved!
6. Upon my flowery breast, Kept wholly for himself alone,
   There he stayed sleeping, and I caressed him,
   And the fanning of the cedars made a breeze.

7. The breeze blew from the turret As I parted his locks;
   With his gentle hand he wounded my neck
   And caused all my senses to be suspended.
8. I remained, lost in oblivion; My face I reclined on the Beloved.
   All ceased and I abandoned myself,
   Leaving my cares forgotten among the lilies.[14]

A person does not have to be a saint to be touched by God. A woman came to me at a conference after I had used St. John's poem, often called "The Dark Night." She had in her hand some verses she had written. Her poem captured for her and for me the same sense of total abandonment to God expressed by John of the Cross. So many profound Christians have led hidden lives and now rest in unvisited graves.

This fine poetic presentation of the encounter with divine Love is Dorothy Foesten's "St. Brigid Talks About Courtship." Foesten beautifully captures the feminine idiom:

I do not trust myself alone with God.
He is so quick to garner me.
I do but glance His way and faith
He swatches off my clothes —
Those garments which I need
To cover up my soul.
And there I stand before Him — naked to the core,
Ashamed and blushing — horrified.
   Would that I could — some fair and favored day
Find courage to approach Him — utterly,
Dropping each loosened figment of disguise,
   And there in swift surrender to His gaze
Know love — and offer simply what I am.
   'Tis not for sham — He keeps on wooing me,
   'Tis me — myself — my Lover-God would have.[15]

The expressions of joy and hope and love that are found in poetry and hymns are innumerable. Francis Thompson, for instance, was an opium derelict selling matches on the streets of London who nonetheless composed poetry. He sent some of his poetry to Alfred Meynell, editor of the journal *Merry England*. Meynell printed one of Thomson's poems, and soon the author appeared in tattered clothes at Meynell's door. Meynell and his wife took the young man in and helped free him of his opium addiction. Thomson became one of the great Christian writers of his time; he wrote the great poem "The Hound of Heaven," portraying divine Love's unceasing search even for those who are fleeing from the Holy One.

John Newton was the captain of a slave ship — one of the most despicable, unchristian jobs that a brutal humankind has ever devised. One night Newton had a dream in which he dropped a sacred ring into the sea from the deck of his ship. Jesus appeared and saw that Newton had lost an incredible treasure. Jesus offered to dive into the water and retrieve this ring — like the ring given the prodigal. John Newton was so moved by this experience that he gave up his slave trading and returned to England to prepare for ministry. He took a parish and wrote some of the finest and most cherished hymns in the English language, among them "Amazing Grace." The grace and love of the risen Christ had been for him *the* amazing grace. The Holy One had touched his heart in a dream.

Not only does the divine Lover seek out scoundrels like Newton and convert them; the Holy also speaks through writers who are not consciously believing Christians. The great German Romantic Johann Wolfgang von Goethe is one stunning example. I know of no better description of divine mercy and redemption than the last scene of Goethe's *Faust*. Faust, the play's hero, has signed a contract with Mephistopheles to give his soul to the devil. He had been given in return any pleasure he desires; he has tasted every human delight. In the final scene Faust is dying and Mephistopheles comes to collect Faust's soul and carry it off to hell. Instead a group of angels sent by Mary, the Mother of Jesus, swoop down from heaven and snatch Faust out of the devil's hand and carry him up to heaven. Among the angels are Gretchen whom Faust betrayed, Mary Magdalene and the woman at the well. As Faust and the angels disappear into the heavens, they are singing, "Those whose seeking never ceases, Are ours for their redeeming." Mahler has set the incomparable poetry of Goethe to the superb music of his Eighth Symphony.[16]

The finest Christian description of afterlife was written by the incomparable Dante. In the midst of the warring city states in Italy in the fourteenth century, the author found himself banished from his beloved Florence in mid-life; in the opening lines of his Divine Comedy, he describes himself in a dark wood, alone and terrified. He is first of all led by the poet Virgil down through the many levels of hell and then is led by Beatrice through purgatory and through the ten realms of heaven to the celestial white rose where he beholds the glory of the triune God. His words fail him. He meets divine Love and he concludes his magnificent vision of heaven with these lines:

> High phantasy lost power and here broke off;
> Yet, as a wheel moves smoothly, free from jars,
> My will and my desire were turned by love,
> The Love that moves the sun and the other stars.[17]

Another example of a poetic vision of the risen Jesus was written by George Herbert, a rural seventeenth century English pastor. It is our concluding picture of love and the Christ. This invitation to sup with the eternal divine Lover has never lost its power. Herbert suggests that we accept the invitation to dine with the risen Jesus:

> Love bade me welcome; yet my soul drew back,
>   Guilty of dust and sin.
> But quick-eyed Love, observing me grow slack
>   From my first entrance in,
> Drew nearer to me, sweetly questioning,
>   If I lacked anything.
>
> "A guest," I answered, "worthy to be here."
>   Love said, "You shall be he."

"I, the unkind, ungrateful? Ah, my dear,
  I cannot look on Thee."
Love took my hand, and smiling did reply,
  "Who made the eyes but I?"

"Truth, Lord, but I have marred them; let my shame
  Go where it doth deserve."
"And know you not," says Love, "who bore the blame?"
  "My dear, then I will serve."
"You must sit down," says Love, "and taste my meat."
  So I did sit and eat.[18]

The Depth and Beauty of Love

After the rain has ceased falling and the sun begins to shine again, a rainbow often appears on the horizon. Few experiences are more moving and beautiful. In the early story of the flood, when Yahweh made a covenant with Noah and the earth that never again would such a catastrophe occur, the sign of this covenant was the bow of color the Creator placed in the cloudy heavens. And our modern scientific understanding actually enhances our sense of wonder at the rainbow. As the white light of the sun passes through the distant raindrops, the light separates into a band of colors; hence, the light of the sun not only makes life on earth possible, it contains every natural color that the human mind can imagine (cf. Gn 13-18). What a wonderful symbol of divine love the light and rainbow are.

Light and love both appear simple. However, the infinite shades of color found in the rainbow show that light is very complex and anything but simple. Similarly, in the Hymn to Love in his First Letter to the Corinthians, Paul shows us the many colors of love, the spectrum of love.

We need not wait for the right kind of a rainstorm to discover the beauty of light. Any of us can pass a beam of light through a glass prism and see spread out before our eyes every color of the rainbow. Not surprisingly, light has become, for humans, a powerful metaphor: Many people have experienced the presence of the Holy One as an ineffable light, a dazzling darkness, or the luminous risen Christ. Light is a mysterious and magnificent splendor. In the late 1800s a devoutly religious scientist, Henry Drummond, compared the many colors of light to the many qualities of love in a little book entitled *The Greatest Thing in the World*.[1]

All modern artists know that blue, yellow and red are the three primary colors; green, orange and purple are the secondary colors. The Holy One weaves these colors into the very fabric of the natural world, into every atom, compound and living thing. Even the most minute particles of matter are named by physicists as three different colors. And love is no less mysterious and wonderful than light. Humans are the only created beings who can share in the Divine's unconditional love and can also return that love to the Creator who made them.

Not only did Jesus tell stories about love being the essence of the nature of the Creator, the Holy Spirit and Paraclete, but he also spoke directly about human love. After washing their feet, he told his disciples to wash one another's feet. He was telling them to assume the position of the lowest servant in a Jewish household. He then said: "I give you a new commandment, that you love one another. *Just as I have loved you, you should love one another. By this everyone will know that you are my disciples, if you have love for one another* " (Jn 13:34-35). Throughout the rest of the New Testament, we find the same emphasis. "Above all, maintain constant love for one another, for love covers a multitude of sins." "God is love and those who abide in love abide in God, and God abides in them." "Those who say, 'I love God' and hate their brothers or sisters are liars."[2]

The finest description of the mysterious depth of love in the New Testament was written by Paul in his First Letter to the Corinthians. We need some background to appreciate his moving Hymn to Love. These words were not written in solitary meditation in the desert; they were written in the heat of turmoil and conflict between Paul and his church in Corinth. Paul had received letters telling him about the factions that had developed in the church, about the chaos in their worship, about immorality condoned within the fellowship. Paul was making very clear to the Corinthian Christians that they were not living the message of Jesus or worshipping in a truly Christian manner.

Corinth was, from the start, an unlikely site for a vital Christian community. In his missionary journeys, Paul had tried to bring the Good News of Jesus' resurrection to the Jewish communities scattered throughout the Asian part of the Roman Empire. But great numbers of Gentiles were also attracted to his teaching. This caused conflict, and Paul and his companions were harried from one place to another until one night Paul had a vision in which he was told to go to Greece. There he was driven from city to city until he came to Corinth, where Gallio, the highly educated Roman Governor of all Greece, told Paul's religious opponents to leave him alone. Confident of religious tolerance, Paul settled down in that wild city for one and a half years.

Corinth was a city of lost souls, and it, like Antioch, was a byword for immorality. Corinth was the seaport crossroad between the Eastern and Western parts of the Roman Empire, and the Greeks, with their proud heritage, chafed under the Roman domination. A large number of Roman legions were stationed in Corinth; sailors came and went, and the Temple of Aphrodite, the goddess of erotic love, provided prostitutes for them. People in this seedy place were hungry for hope, and the message of Christianity filled the void within them. Paul turned no one away, and the fellowship grew day by day. People of every walk of life filled the Church: rich merchants, solid citizens and Roman soldiers, the poor and sick, the mentally imbalanced, and prostitutes sick of their way of life. It is little wonder that problems arose when Paul left Greece and returned to Asia Minor.

Paul's letter comes from a troubled heart; he was pleading with the Church members to heal their factions, to provide for the poor at their communal suppers and eucharists, to restrain their erotic impulses, to use their gifts of the spirit — considered the manifestations of the Holy Spirit — with discretion. In this letter Paul names one group of these gifts: healing, revelations, discernment of spirits, gifts of wisdom and knowledge, tongue speaking and prophecy. While presenting this list of gifts or "charisms" and his directions on how to use them (which occurs in Chapter 14), Paul suddenly breaks into a lyric description of Love. He exhorts the Corinthians to seek the gifts of the spirit, but then he writes that he will now show what really makes any human or divine gift valuable: LOVE. He says that he will show them "the most extraordinary reality that undergirds and is the essence of the Christians' pathway through life."[3] Here are Paul's words:

> If I speak in the tongues of mortals and of angels, but do not have love, I am a noisy gong or a clanging cymbal. And if I have prophetic powers, and understand all mysteries and all knowledge, and if I have all faith, so as to remove mountains, but do not have love, I am nothing. If I give away all my possessions, and if I hand over my body so that I may boast, but do not have love, I gain nothing.
>
> Love is patient; love is kind; love is not envious or boastful or arrogant or rude. It does not insist on its own way; it is not irritable or resentful; it does not rejoice in wrongdoing, but rejoices in the truth. It bears all things, believes all things, hopes all things, endures all things.
>
> Love never ends. But as for prophecies, they will come to an end; as for tongues, they will cease; as for knowledge, it will come to an end. For we know only in part, and we prophesy only in part; but when the complete comes, the partial will come to an end. When I was a child, I spoke like a child, I thought like a child, I reasoned like a child; when I became an adult, I put an end to childish ways. For now we see in a mirror, dimly, but then we will see face to face. Now I know only in part; then I will know fully, even as I have been fully known. And now faith, hope, and love abide, these three; and the greatest of these is love.

Love — The Foundation of All Genuine Religious Practice and Value

Everything that we do, Paul says, needs to be rooted and grounded in love. And Paul describes in detail the qualities that are part and parcel of love. Jesus told the story of a priest and Levite who passed by a dying man on the road to Jericho; they were deeply religious men, but they let their fear overcome their love. In his Hymn to Love, Paul passes love through the prism of his Christian soul and describes distinctive attributes of the love that he had experienced from the risen Jesus.

All gifts, both human and spiritual, have no value unless they manifest the love of Jesus, who came among us as a baby in a stable, lived among us, suffered with us, suffered for us and opened the gates of eternal life to us. Paul makes his meaning very clear:

Having the gift of ecstatic speech is good, but unless we use it to show love to other people, our utterance becomes a lot of meaningless noise.

We may have prophetic powers and be able to reveal the hidden meanings of life and even foretell the future, but if these are not used in love and for love, we are nothing at all.

We can know all human knowledge, even spiritual mysteries, but if these gifts are lacking in love, these marvelous capacities can lead us astray. These things without love are merely dust and ashes.

Faith is a great gift and the source of much healing in Jesus' ministry. However, if we have faith enough to remove mountains and do it only to show our power, rather than to show that divine Love is flowing through us, we gain nothing and are nothing.

We can even give away all of our human wealth and possessions to feed the poor, and yet, if we do it to absolve our own guilt, to follow religious law, or to gain admiration from others, we have done nothing of worth. These gifts are spiritually valuable only as we give them from an overflowing, loving heart.

We can even sacrifice our lives, our very bodies; if, however, we do it so we can boast or gain fame and honor, we gain absolutely nothing.[4]

We may get so caught up with Paul's negative statements about these human and divine gifts that we forget that these gifts can be good. Francis Whiting has pointed out that we can turn these negative statements into positive ones without changing the meaning:

If I speak in the tongues of mortals and of angels, and have love, I am not a noisy gong or a clanging cymbal. And if I have prophetic powers, and understand all mysteries and all knowledge, and if I have all faith, so as to remove mountains, and have love, I am something. If I give away all my possessions, and if I hand over my body to be sacrificed and do it with love, I gain something.[5]

In other words, love empowers and alone gives eternal value to the gifts that the Creator has given us.

In his Letter to the Romans Paul was writing to a Church he had never visited. His message in this letter is similar to his message to the Corinthians. He writes of other gifts, gifts that many of us take for granted, and he applies the same rule to these gifts. He advises the Romans not to become inflated about the gifts they have. After mentioning prophecy in a positive way and again and again, Paul lists other gifts and suggests that they be used with humility and love:

If we have the gift of serving others, ministering as a deacon, let us use this ability to the full and in love.

When we have the gift of teaching, we need to put our full energy and knowledge into this gift and teach with love. When we are gifted with the ability to preach the good news, let us give our time and energy to developing that gift and to practicing it with love.

Those who have the ability to listen to, to comfort, to console those who are in need, let them exercise this gift with understanding and gentleness — in other words, in love.

Those who have the capacity to give generously and those who have been given the gift of many worldly possessions, let these people give generously and with a glad heart, in the spirit of love, anonymously.

You have born leaders among you; let them take up the position of leadership even though this role is difficult. Good leaders will reconcile those they lead. Let them do this with diligence and love. A Church without such leaders will be in trouble.

Those who have the capacity to show mercy and compassion need to seek out the lost and forgotten and sick and share the mercy and love of Jesus with them.[6]

Paul was speaking not only to the Church in Rome that he did not know, but also to all of us today, all who wish to have true religious fellowship with one another. Real fellowship, Paul asserts, is grounded in love. And Peter agrees. Soon after he reminds us that love covers most sins, Peter affirms Paul's words on love: "Like good stewards of the manifold grace of God, serve one another with whatever gift each of you has received. Whoever speaks must do so as one who is speaking the very words of God; whoever serves must do it with the strength that God supplies"; Peter is speaking of the very love that Paul describes so well (cf. 1 Pt 4:10-11).

Love Itself

I was reminded of Henry Drummond's list of nine distinctive qualities of love in his pamphlet *The Greatest Thing in the World*, based on 1 Corinthians 13, when several years ago a woman at a conference came up to me and gave me her own much longer list. I read the woman's fifteen descriptions of love to the group, who had gathered together to meditate on achieving growth in love. Many of the group wanted copies of this list, and I have used it again and again with the same result. What follows is a greatly expanded version of this woman's spectrum of love, based on a month's study of Paul's magnificent Greek.[7]

Love Is . . .

Patient: Endures trials and bears pains calmly; can wait until the time is ripe; never gives up; is never picky or demanding; does not have expectations of others; deals without defensiveness with conflict and criticism even when they seem unfair.

Kind: Is thoughtful; has a gentle, helpful, considerate nature; is sympathetic; compassionate; merciful; worthy; good; useful; understanding and affectionate where it is proper.

Attentive: Listens to others with patience; sees the value of others and of the Holy One who dwells in them; knows that only as we listen to others and share their burdens can we bring healing to them.

Consoling: Recognizes the pain of grief and sorrow of others and reaches out to them; is therefore compassionate to them; is willing to be with suffering, dying, bereaved people.

Confident: Is not jealous, envious or possessive; is not fearful of losing the affection and concern of others or of the divine; friendly; is secure in the knowledge that all will be well in the end.

Modest: Is not boastful; not puffed up; not overbearing; not given to excessive pride; proper; reserved; unobtrusive; does not wish to be showy or to be the center of attention; is not a wind bag.

Humble: Is not arrogant or proud; not overbearing; not overly convinced of one's own importance; treats all others as human beings of equal value; knows all of us have sometimes failed; is not pushy or judgmental.

Gracious: Is never rude; honors the attitudes and feelings of others; does not behave offensively or in an unseemly manner; is not ill-mannered; is polite, courteous and proper.

Considerate: Is yielding and flexible; thoughtful; willing and able to listen; does not insist on or persist in pressing for or demanding one's own way; does not have expectations; is not selfish, self-seeking or self-centered.

Good-natured: Is not easily stirred up to wrath; not irritable; not easily angered; not touchy or ill-tempered; not easily annoyed or exasperated; is easygoing; does not lose its head.

Forgiving: Excuses the faults of others; does not have paroxysms[8] of rage; keeps no record of wrong even on oneself; is not resentful; is not inclined to feel bitterness or resentment; does not hold grudges; sees no human beings as faultless; does not keep a tally of evils, injuries and nastiness.

Joyful: Has joy in the righteous and kind; delights in the holy and knows the truth; is jubilant when good appears; exalts in song and praise and love; never rejoices in the wrong or ugly or devious; is never happy about those who suffer evil or injustice.

Playful: Is merry (as if always celebrating the great cosmic drama of Christmas); does not take itself too seriously; enjoys a playful interchange with human beings; never revels in darkness, depression and dejection.

Forbearing: Puts up with and bears difficulties; persists when all seems hopeless; bears up under rejection; covers over the faults of others; keeps confidences; does not judge; does not gossip; does not complain about hardships.[9]

Believing: Trusts and accepts the truth; is open-minded to new truth; has a firm conviction that a loving Creator has made our universe and us; is always hoping to find truthfulness and goodness in others; does not project faults on others; is not overly doubtful or suspicious.

Hopeful: Is encouraging; nurturing; always expects the best in others (without being naïve); looks forward to healthy goals with expectation of fulfillment; never expects the worst nor is happy with pessimism; is

	expectant; looks for good in this world and the world to come; foresees the good.
Enduring:	Is faithful and steadfast; carries through in spite of difficulties and hardships; stands firm when others flee; never gives up hope for self, others or the world; waits with solid confidence for divine help.
Endless:	Is eternal; goes on forever, world without end; endures without limit; never ends; is divine, holy, Godlike; never drifts off course; never fails, loses or weakens.

Meditating on Paul's words in his Ode to Love has greatly widened my knowledge of the meaning of love and of Paul's intimate personal knowledge of the greatest quality of life — the mystery of divine and human love. I began to see more clearly that Paul is presenting the essential message of Jesus found in the four gospels. Paul's thirteen verses provide a summary of the beatitudes and the Sermon on the Mount, of the Lord's Prayer, the Apostles' Creed and even of Jesus' parables. The letters of Paul were sent before any of the gospels were written; Paul was in touch with the early Church's coherent body of common knowledge about Jesus and his teaching. In the deepest matters of faith, the letters of Paul, the four gospels, and the Acts of the Apostles all display the same understanding of the good news of the Christian way and affirm the historical reality of Jesus, of Jesus' teaching and resurrection, of the supreme historical example of love's eternity.

We have already noted that the slave-ridden and poverty-stricken Roman world was hungering for a message of hope. Life was barren for the slaves and the displaced common people. The idea of a self-giving God who cared enough to come among human beings as a historical human person in a specific time, to teach them, suffer with them, be crucified and rise again for them, *was a totally new religious idea to that world.* No wonder that Jesus and his apostles were received with such enthusiasm by the downtrodden and anxious people of that time. I know of no other description of the significance and the eternal value of love in the ancient Western world comparable to verses four to nine of Paul's Hymn to Love. Now we consider each of these elements of love one by one in greater depth.

Love Is Patient

We have already looked at the incredible patience of the father to his wayward and impudent sons. Love seldom forces issues; it waits until the time is right. The Eternal One does not have to be impatient. The Holy One patiently accepted the birth in a manger, life as a refugee in Egypt, the opposition of religious leaders, and the Roman crucifixion, and then this Holy One displayed the eternal strength of love in the resurrection and the appearance of the risen Jesus to his disciples and to those with special needs from that day to this.[10] One of the finest descriptions of the necessity of patience in achieving love is found in the words of Father Zossima in Dostoyevsky's *The Brothers Karamazov*. He is addressing not another monk but a flighty middle-class woman who is complaining about the difficulty of achieving growth in love. Father Zossima takes the woman seriously and replies patiently:

> Never be afraid of your petty selfishness when you try to achieve love, and don't be too alarmed if you act badly on occasion. I'm sorry I cannot tell you anything more reassuring. A true act of love, unlike imaginary love, is hard and forbidding. Imaginary love yearns for an immediate heroic act that is achieved quickly and seen by everyone. People may actually reach a point where they are willing to sacrifice their lives, as long as the ordeal doesn't take too long, is quickly over — just like on the stage, with the public watching and admiring. A true act of love, on the other hand, requires hard work and patience, and, for some, it is a whole way of life. But I predict that at the very moment when you see despairingly that, despite all your efforts, you have not only failed to come closer to your goal but, indeed, seem even farther from it than ever — at that very moment, you

will have achieved your goal and will recognize the miraculous power of our Lord, who has always loved you and has secretly guided you all along.[11]

Love Is Kind

Dostoyevsky's Father Zossima is not only patient, he is the essence of kindness. The qualities of love overlap each other, but in some actions one facet shines more brightly than others. We may never know until eternity how much one kind act has touched and even transformed another person. Oscar Wilde tells in his memoirs of such an act of kindness that happened to him when he was in prison for a crime considered heinous in his day. He was led from prison to face the indignities of the Court of Bankruptcy:

> When I was brought down from my prison between two policemen, [a man I know] waited in the long dreary corridor so that, before the whole crowd, whom an action so sweet and simple hushed into silence, he might gravely raise his hat to me, as, handcuffed and with bowed head, I passed him by. Men have gone to heaven for smaller things than that. I do not know to the present moment whether he is aware that I was even conscious of his action. I store it in the treasure-house of my heart. When wisdom has been profitless to me, philosophy barren, and the proverbs and phrases of those who have sought to give me consolation as dust and ashes in my mouth, the memory of that little, lovely, silent act of love has unsealed for me all the wells of pity, and brought me out of the bitterness of lonely exile into harmony with the wounded, broken, and great heart of the world.[12]

Few of us can express ourselves as eloquently as Oscar Wilde, but most of us have experienced situations in which we have received kindness that has touched us this deeply or even changed our lives. In order to become instruments of this depth of kindness, we need to have experienced it from some other human being or directly from the divine Lover. Paul, for instance, had a direct experience of the divine while traveling on a Damascus road, and he was changed from an apostle of hatred to an apostle of love. Although Freud stated that such apparent experiences of religion and God are simply projections of our relationships with our human parents, the great theologian, Baron von Hügel proposed an alternative view. Von Hügel studied the life of a famous atheist, and he pointed out that the man's parents had been so cold and unloving that he could not have believed in a loving divinity. According to von Hügel, the Creator fashioned the intimate human family as a loving place where we might receive an intimation of divine love. Several of the finest modern scientific thinkers have come to von Hügel's position; the whole of the universe, they have inferred, was created to produce human beings so that they might know the Creator and unconditional love.[13]

Augustine wrote that God made us restless so that we might find our rest in the Holy One. He also wrote that if there had been only one lost human being in the world, God in Jesus would still have been born in a manger, have suffered with that one individual, and have died on a cross and risen from the dead to open the gates of eternity — all for that *one person*. When we truly realize that the Holy One loves each of us with that kind of unconditional kindness, we begin to see how we need to treat one another. In his parable of the sheep and goats, Jesus explains the necessity of reaching with kindness to our brothers and sisters, for when we do we are being kind of Jesus himself.

Jesus was very concrete in describing how we are to show kindness. We are to offer food to the hungry, a cup of cold water to the thirsty, welcome and homes to the strangers and homeless, clothes to the naked; we are to care for the sick with loving kindness, to visit those in prison and to give them understanding and consolation. When we are involved in these actions of kindness, we are performing them for Jesus himself. Jesus assumed that we would give the same kindness to our families and friends (cf. Mt 25:31-40; 5:46-47).

Jesus knew his scripture well, and his words echo in a personal way the words of Isaiah (58:6-9):

> Is not this the fast that I choose:
>> to loose the bonds of injustice,
>> to undo the thongs of the yoke,
> to let the oppressed go free,
>> and to break every yoke?
> Is it not to share your bread with the hungry,
>> and bring the homeless poor into your house;
> when you see the naked, to cover them,
>> and not to hide yourself from your own kin?
> Then your light shall break forth like the dawn,
>> and your healing shall spring up quickly;
> your vindicator shall go before you,
>> the glory of the LORD shall be your rear guard.
> Then you shall call, and the LORD will answer;
>> you shall cry for help, and he will say, Here I am.

Catherine of Siena, one of the most influential Christians of the Middle Ages, gave the same advice to one of her nuns who had asked what she could do to repay God for all the grace that had been showered upon her. Catherine wrote: "Give someone unworthy of your kindness and love the same measure of thoughtful care and kindness that God has given you."[14]

Love Is Attentive and Willing to Listen

These words are not specifically listed in the Greek, but they are implied in patience and kindness. Some people find it easy to listen while others find it difficult. Nonetheless, nearly everyone with the desire can *learn* to be attentive to other people and to listen to them. We cannot have loving kindness toward others unless we see them as they are. Very few of us are really secure and confident — no matter what face we present to the world. When we are attentive to another, we try to listen to the depth of another soul. We try to remove our projections, our jealousy. We accompany the other and follow his or her lead. As we do this, we truly value the other. We focus on him or her and try to put our own agenda aside. The other person is there and real. I know of a young child who was with her two parents at a restaurant. As the waitress was about to take the child's order, the mother spoke up: "She will have a hamburger." But the waitress said: "No, I am asking the little girl." The child replied: "Gee, I am real." Many of us older folks have a young child in us who needs to be noticed as real and listened to.

Listening takes attention and patience. We cannot love those to whom we will not listen; we do not know who they really are or what they want and need. Real kindness requires giving to others what they need, not what we think that they need. When Ollie Backus, a skilled teacher and psychologist, came to St. Luke's Church as director of religious education, she observed our church school. At our first staff meeting together, she said: "It would be better if we eliminated the program. The teachers are not listening to the children. We cannot teach love unless we practice it; we cannot love anyone to whom we have not listened. It will take five years to train the teachers to practice the Christian love they are trying to teach."

My most remarkable experience of listening occurred many years ago in my office; I discovered that "listening" can, paradoxically, mean accepting another's silence. A man made an hour appointment to see me. He arrived on time. We shook hands and he greeted me as I welcomed him. We sat down in chairs facing each other. I asked him what he wanted to talk about. I sat quietly waiting for him to speak. Ten minutes went by without a word, half an hour passed. Finally our hour was over. The man got up from his chair, came over to me, took me by the hand and said: "You will never know what this hour has meant to me. I did not think that anyone could abide my presence for an hour without words." James Baldwin was right: When we stop listening to one another, the light goes out.

Love Is Consoling

Many people around us are bearing much more pain and sorrow than we realize. (Television reveals the pain ordinary people suffer. Talk shows, for instance, bring the suffering and cruelty of the world into our very living rooms and bedrooms.) If we are active followers of Jesus Christ and of love, we find that we are called to be compassionate with those who come to us. People began to come and see me without my having announced that I would listen or was ready to listen. When I told Jung this experience, he observed, "When your unconscious is ready, the unconscious of other people will know it and people will come to you."

As we deal with our darkness and learn to listen, those needing compassion will come to us. Indeed, one major problem is that we often do not set limits and have referral sources, and then we can be overwhelmed. We need to find out how much of others' suffering we can bear. One of the heavy burdens of helping professionals — doctors, clergy, counselors, serious Christians, teachers, social workers — is carrying the vast burdens of darkness and pain in the world. Jung would work for three months and then take a month off in order to cleanse himself of the depression and pain he had absorbed.

Of course, we need to be sensitive and consoling to our families and close friends and to ourselves. Then we need to discern when we are helping others by listening ourselves, and when we need to refer them to someone else. When I was twenty-one my mother was taken terminally ill. I was living at college three hundred miles away. Each weekend for four months I traveled back and forth through ice and rain and snow to see her. No one else made such consistent visits to her; her appreciation was boundless. I learned what it meant to give, knowing that I soon would not have access to her caring presence. This was one of my best preparations for ministry. If I could be with her in her dying, then I could be with anyone. I had learned how much a caring presence can mean to another.

One of the reasons so few people will visit the dying is that they have not faced their own mortality. Too few of us are given a view of reality that provides an understanding or picture of our continuing life after death. Too many of us have not seen the incredible meaning of Jesus' birth, teachings and resurrection. We become so fearful of death that we dare not look at it. We cannot bring consolation to the dying unless we have a vision of life beyond death; the dying can read our minds and souls. Through his loving presence, Francis of Assisi reminded us that consolation was a part of love and that dying is the doorway to eternal life.[15]

We are most likely to give consolation to the suffering and dying when our patient listening is supported by kindness and compassion and a conviction that life is not conquered by death. The threads of the tapestry of love are interwoven with each other.

Love Is Trusting

Sometimes it is helpful to describe something by what it is not. Endless strings of words never fully tell everything about any real experience. For example, what looks like simple garden dirt contains dozens of chemicals, and each of those chemicals contain atoms. And each of these tiny blocks of matter contain subatomic particles that baffle the greatest scientists of our time. Even something as ordinary as the taste of blue cheese is impossible to convey to one who has never eaten it. So it is not surprising that Paul cannot fully describe the qualities of love, which are the very essence of God. Paul reminds us that the truly loving person must settle for partial understanding, secure in the knowledge and faith that in the end love conquers every obstacle. People with this conviction can afford to take their time and be relaxed, calm and friendly, and reach out to others. They have no need to be defensive, controlling, demanding their own way, bigoted. They need not envy other people. If we live in love and do our best, we know that the Holy One is in charge, and in the end all will be well.

William Wilberforce is a perfect example of trusting security. In a small evangelical prayer meeting in London, he received the insight that slavery was wrong, counter to the essential view of Jesus and of God. He was a man of means and had time to do with his life what he was certain was right. He entered the political arena and was elected in the late eighteenth century to Parliament. For thirty years he introduced each year a bill that would abolish slavery in the British Empire. Each year his bill was voted down. He was not fearful or anxious; he trusted his religious insight. He died and the next year Parliament finally passed the bill he had first introduced so many years before. Agape love is never pushy; it is persistent, but it does not coerce others by violence or force.

Love Is Modest

Pride is one of the cardinal failings of human beings. Deep in most of us is the wish to be the center of things and have others admire our accomplishments. Paul said that he would boast only of his weakness. The loving person is modest, not wanting to be at the center of the stage and almost embarrassed by attention. Modest women and men are well aware that most of the saints have spoken of their own inadequacies, of their flaws and weaknesses. Modest people realize that any creative good they do by word or deed occurs not only through their own effort but because the spirit of love, the Holy Spirit, is working through them. So they are not braggarts or windbags.

Jesus said that when we give alms, we should do it unobtrusively, secretly. When we pray, we should do it in private, with the doors closed. When we fast, we are not to let the world know that we are fasting; we need to appear to be at our brightest and best. Those who boast about their worldly accomplishments are deceived, and those who brag about their religious accomplishments are hypocrites. The fact that Augustus Caesar is remembered today is largely because Jesus of Nazareth — whose life and teaching were a model of modesty — was born in his reign, not because he created an empire that has vanished. The genuine religious practice of love outlasts empires — a sobering thought.

John Woolman had been educated to be a clerk, an important figure in the early days of colonial America since many people at that time could not read or write. Woolman realized that his profession would require that he make out bills of sale for slaves. But he was a Quaker and had a deep conviction that had come to him in a Friends Meeting: Human beings, he realized, have no right under God or love to buy and sell each other. Woolman became a tailor; at least this profession would do no one harm. He wandered up and down the thirteen colonies making clothes and attending the weekly Meetings of the Society of Friends. At all these meetings he shared his spiritual insight. When he died some forty years later, no Quaker in the Colonies owned a slave.

Love Is Humble

Neither humility nor modesty is very popular in our secular society. Yet, the opposite of arrogant, pushy, judging, overbearing behavior is humility. Jesus spoke again and again about humility. One of Jesus' greatest and most radical ideas was that each and every human being has infinite value.

During the Cultural Revolution in China, some soldiers were burning copies of the New Testament. One of them wondered what could be so dangerous in these books. He saved one book and read it. He realized for the first time in his life that every human being might have infinite worth and value. He sought out the Christians to learn more; his deep longing for this insight was satisfied. Like the early Christians, he found other people who treated each other as equals. They loved one another. Soon after the Cultural Revolution, I visited a church in Canton. It had been open only a few months; it was packed with old and young singing with an enthusiasm worthy of the early Church. Their fellowship had not been destroyed by oppression.

In his Letter to the Philippians (2:5-11), Paul gives the classic description of humble self-giving:

Let the same mind be in you that was in Christ Jesus, who, though he was in the form of God, did not regard equality with God as something to be exploited, but emptied himself, taking the form of a slave, being born in human likeness. And being found in human form, he humbled himself and became obedient to the point of death — even death on a cross.

Therefore God also highly exalted him and gave him the name that is above every name, so that at the name of Jesus every knee should bend, in heaven and on earth and under the earth, and every tongue should confess that Jesus Christ is Lord, to the glory of God the Father.

Love Is Gracious

It is difficult to find a word that conveys the quality opposite to rudeness, unseemliness, shamefulness, dishonor, disgrace. The English word that fits best for me is "gracious." *Grace* is a combination of beauty, kindness, goodness. The Holy One is gracious. The Creator gives, expecting nothing in return; the Divine gives grace unexpectedly and freely, with no demands, no strings attached. Jesus was born into the world not because we deserved his coming. He came to us as a free gift before most human beings had ever thought of turning to the Divine.

"Gracious" also implies coordination, smoothness of movement or action. The gracious one is not shocked or disturbed by what others reveal about themselves. The entire universe in its infinite complexity is the gracious creation from which life and consciousness and graciousness can evolve. And real graciousness, like love, can never be given as a list of rules. Indeed, sometimes graciousness requires that we break some old custom — but never just for shock value. The real reason for good manners is to prevent unnecessary hurt or wounds.

Graciousness is never violent. The purpose of nonviolent movements is to effect change without losing the values toward what we wish to move. Mandela and de Klerk, both deeply devout, practicing Christians, were acting from love and were gracious and forgiving, and because of them political transformation has taken place in South Africa to a remarkable degree.

When I taught in a nonviolence program at Notre Dame, we discovered that many students came into the program for violent reasons. So we instituted classes in which students in the program could look at their own inner violence. We wanted them to realize that true nonviolence is *gracious*. Graciousness can confront when it is appropriate. Jesus was the essence of graciousness at a party held by one of the leading Pharisees, where he was not treated with customary courtesy. No servant had been instructed to wash Jesus' feet, and Jesus was not given the customary, courteous kiss of peace. Then, during the men's dinner (at which women were present only to serve the men), a woman of the street — defying all custom — broke into the room where the men reclined at dinner. Paying no attention to the shock and scorn of the men, the woman stood behind Jesus and bathed his feet with tears, wiped them with her hair and anointed them with oil.

Jesus noticed the indignation and critical attitude of his host and told him a parable: There were, he said, two debtors, one with insignificant debts, the other with a staggering debt. Both were forgiven. Jesus asked his Pharisee host which debtor would be more grateful. When the Pharisee replied that he supposed it would be the one with the greater debt, Jesus said: "Therefore, I tell you, her sins, which were many, have been forgiven; hence she has shown great love." Then he sent the woman off with words of forgiveness, with a blessing, and with praise for the great love she had shown. At this party, then, Jesus found a way to be both graciously kind to the woman and graciously assertive to the host.

Jesus also showed similar graciousness to the woman dragged before him for adultery. Jesus simply said, "Let anyone among you who is without sin be the first to throw a stone at her." Then he bent over and wrote in the sand until her accusers left one by one. When they were alone, he said: "Neither do I condemn you" (Lk 7:36-50; Jn 8:3-11).

Love Is Adaptable

The human species has flourished on earth largely because it is adaptable to changing conditions. Love is the ultimate in adaptation. When we love, we adapt to all levels of reality. If we are to grow, we need to keep on seeking until we find the utter fulfillment and joy of eternal life. We can continue the journey only when we are flexible, pliant, adaptable. Too often we get caught on the infantile level of demanding that we have our own way. (Many marriages sound like the sandbox squabbles of three-year-olds.) Only human love can lead us through the various stages of human development from infancy to full spiritual maturity in eternal fellowship with divine Love. But it is difficult to teach others the need for a willingness to seek and grow toward wholeness, because we who are teaching need to be on our own way toward that goal. We can lead others no further than we have gone ourselves.

Many have written on human growth and development, but few of these writers describe the final goal of preparing for eternity. Experts on human development tell us that the infant needs unconditional love, which lays a secure foundation for the rest of life. In order to grow, the young child also needs to learn loving, reasonable limits. When school-age children are given a warm and fair environment, they soak up knowledge like a sponge and usually pick up their parents' values. Then comes adolescence, a time when children learn to find their own way, learn to deal with the world around them. Then, as they reach adulthood, they begin to explore real relationship and develop a way of making a living. Only loving, adaptable parents can lead their children toward that kind of growth. Nonetheless, even the stage of relationship and career is not the final human goal, and without wise and loving examples adults can easily get caught in this stage and move no further.

The materialistic, secular world in which we live does not satisfy all our deepest needs. Many people in their forties pass through a mid-life crisis, because there is no ultimate meaning within the purely secular world. Caring and understanding people who have passed beyond this purely secular view can guide others to another stage of development; by loving concern they can lead others to experience the mystical reality of love that is the ultimate foundation of all reality. Those who make this transition often find golden years in which they can be more alive and creative than they have ever been before. The last stage of old age need not be dismal. It can be a time when we pause and reflect and prepare for the eternal life and eternal love that lie ahead. Any study of human development that does not deal with this final adaptation, this wonderful final stage, does not understand the essential mystery of human life.[16]

Love Is Good-natured

Paul writes again and again of the need to be in control of our emotions. We do not have self-control when we are prone to blowing up at other people, to having "paroxysms" of rage. (Again note that the word that Paul uses is a Greek word; when the Greek letters of the word are replaced by English ones, the word still has the same English meaning.) We are not letting love rule us when we are as irritable and disagreeable as tired children. We are not good-natured when we are touchy, ill-tempered (particularly with those closest to us). In a later chapter, we will deal more fully with the roots of our nasty behavior and how we can control it, but here are some suggestions:

1. We need to recognize that we are not living in love when we dump our angry emotions on other people.

2. This does not mean repressing our inner angers, frustration, pain and hurt. We can never change anything in ourselves that we do not face. We need to face our irritation, anger and hurt; but we do not need to project this onto other people, whether it be family, friend, stranger or enemy.

3. We need time to stop and reflect in silence. Keeping track of one's explosions in a notebook or journal can remind us of how far we still have to go.

4. Other people or situations may trigger our reactions, but
these are *our* reactions, and it is seldom creative to let them
out on others until we have paused to consider what response
on our part will be appropriate and good-natured and loving.

A discussion of love's good nature brings us to one of the brightest colors in the spectrum of love: forgiveness.

Love Is Forgiving

Love does not calculate, does not keep a record or accounting
of other people's hurtful actions. Unfortunately, there is a lot of
evil in our world. Many actions are cruel and destructive; many
events are ugly, terrible, pernicious. Love, however, does not
mull over these things again and again; love does not hold
grudges, does not ponder them, dwell on them, hang onto them.
Love never gossips about other people's faults. Jesus gave specific
instruction on this subject to his disciples when Peter asked if he
should forgive seven times. Jesus replied: "No, seventy times
seven" — by which he meant, "infinitely." Love conquered evil
on the cross as Jesus cried out: "Father, forgive them for they
know not what they do." Jesus rose again to let us know that evil
does not have the last word. And his disciples followed his way.
As Stephen was being stoned, he cried out: "Lord, do not hold
this sin against them." Observing these forgiving Christians, the
pagan world was incredulous. Hundreds, thousands of men and
women were thrown into the arena to face wild beasts or worse,
yet these people died forgiving those who betrayed them, who
judged them, and who drove them into the arena. And in three
hundred years the spirit of these people conquered the destroy-
ers and took over the Roman Empire. They lived the prayer Jesus
gave them. They prayed: Forgive us our trespassers as we forgive
those who trespass against us.

Love is never proud about holding grudges. Sixty years ago I
was talking to an older person in our boarding house. Suddenly
this person held up a skinny, crooked finger and said with
delight: "This is the sign that I never forget or forgive anyone who

injures me or has slighted me. I never forgive." I was chilled by the comment, and I can still hear the cold rasping voice that uttered these words. I was young and naïve, but I knew something was terribly wrong.

During the blitz on London during World War II, Charles Williams wrote a little book entitled *On Forgiveness of Sins*. In it this profound Christian summarizes the theme of his many novels and poetic works. I paraphrase his conclusions. There are things, he says, that need not be forgiven: actions done to us that seem nasty or unfair, but that actually reflect our misunderstanding of the other person (such events are not rare when we are angry). There are things that ought to be forgiven: real hurts that have been inflicted on us by others, whether close friends or strangers. There are also some actions that can't be forgiven; Williams was referring to the death and destruction the blitz had created. However, Williams concludes that the real Christian needs to forgive even these things — just as Christ did on the cross.

A close friend of mine had been deeply hurt as a young man by one he thought he could trust. He was finally able to tell me about it. The incident continued to haunt and consume him until a minister suggested that he write a letter to God in which he offered forgiveness to the individual. He gave me permission to use this letter.

> Dear Heavenly Father, Creator of Life and Love,
>
> Please take my anger and hatred I feel toward John. I place my feelings into the cup of salvation which Jesus created with his death and resurrection. Transform my feelings into a positive, creative source of energy which I will use to help implement your will on earth.
>
> Eternal One, please set John free of what afflicts him. John, I completely and without reservation forgive you. I set you free of my anger. When I think of you and feel my anger, I will remind myself of Christ's forgiveness and compassion. I pray for you and wish you well.

God, I ask you for your special help in my journey. I long
to live life as your Son Jesus exemplifies it. Please open my
heart to your love. This I ask in Jesus' name,

Your son, Carl

A few nights after writing this letter, Carl dreamed that he saw
his hurt and anger poured into the chalice of Christ's blood. From
that time on forgiveness gradually replaced his continued concern with the injury done to him.

Love Is Joyful

Joy is one of the distinguishing marks of all the real saints.
Christianity is the most joyful religion of humankind; Christians
affirm that in the end all will be well and the divine will continue
to woo all of us through all eternity. Yet we also know that evil
exists in our universe and in the human heart. Why is there evil
in a world created by divine Love? The Holy One knew that only
free human and angelic beings could respond to Love with
genuine caring and love. Love never forces itself on anyone; we
are free *not to allow* divine Love to touch us and give us joy. When
we reject love, we fall into the company of those angelic powers
that revolted against God because they believed that power and
force alone could run the world. Through crucifixion, resurrection, ascension, Jesus Christ conquered the Evil One and opened
the gates of heaven to all who truly wish to seek it.[17] As we open
ourselves to the presence of this saving One in quiet and prayer,
we can know the joy of heaven even in the midst of the worst
adversity.

"Love is never glad or happy in unrighteousness, in wicked-
ness, or injustice or injury, but rejoices from the bottom of its heart
with the truth: with righteousness, honesty, with genuine reality."[18] Love never takes any pleasure in the wrong. When people
enjoy giving prophecies of doom, they are straying from the basic
truth of the good news of Jesus of Nazareth. But love drives us
to seek truth and righteousness in every area of life. Love is also

free; again, something is amiss when anyone tries to force us to believe what we do not believe. Brainwashing is evil.

Love Is Playful

When we are joyful, we want to dance and sing. The Hebrews had a great song book, the psalms. Likewise, only a minute number of Christians do not sing when they come together. My heart is lifted every time I hear a gathering of Christians sing with joy:

> Love Divine, all loves excelling,
> Joy of heaven, to earth come down,
> Fix in us thy humble dwelling,
> All thy faithful mercies crown!

Some of the greatest music, poetry, art and sculpture has bubbled out of the response to the drama of Christmas and Easter. When we look at this incredible world of rainbows and sunsets, of mountains and lake-filled valleys, of the boundless varieties of flowers of the field and fish of the sea, we are looking at the playfulness of God. Van Gogh wrote that his magnificent pictures were inspired by the love he beheld in nature and honest human affection; he beheld the Creator when he looked out on a sunlit field or human face.

When we are unduly serious and cannot relish our play and delight, we can cut ourselves off from the radiant unconditional joy and playfulness of God.

John Masefield catches the spirit of this gracious, joyful, playful Creator:

> Love and be merry, remember, better the world with a song,
> Better the world with a blow in the teeth of a wrong.
> Laugh, for the time is brief, a thread the length of a span.
> Laugh and be proud to belong to the old proud pageant
>   of man.

Laugh and be merry; remember, in olden time
God made Heaven and Earth for joy he took in a rhyme,
Made them, and filled them full with the strong red wine
   of his mirth
The splendid joy of the stars: the joy of the earth.

So we must laugh and drink from the deep blue cup of
   the sky,
Join the jubilant song of the great stars sweeping by,
Laugh, and battle, and work, and drink of the wine
   outpoured
In the dear green earth, the sign of the joy of the Lord.

Laugh and be merry together, like brothers akin,
Guesting awhile in the rooms of a beautiful inn.
Glad till the dancing stops, and the lilt of the music ends.
Laugh till the game is played, and be you merry,
   my friends.[19]

Love Is Forbearing, Believing, Hopeful and Enduring

These four words belong together. They express the courageous, persistent, faithful and hopeful character of the persecuted Christian fellowship — the Church that eventually
outlasted and took over the Roman Empire. They stood fast
because they believed that they had experienced the kingdom of
heaven here on earth. They were convinced (conquered by) the
reality of their vision of a loving Abba who had met them in Jesus,
the teacher from Nazareth; he had also appeared to them risen
from the dead. As the disciples met together after Jesus' resurrection, new spiritual understanding and healing love was
poured on them and through them. Meeting secretly in the
catacombs or in secluded private homes, they experienced the
presence of the risen Jesus in their eucharist and received a
greater portion of the Holy Spirit. Many of these men and women
met their death in the arena singing hymns of faith and joy and
confidence. The pagan world looked on in amazement. The blood
of martyrs was indeed the seed of the Church.

Those of us with nominal commitment who have taken Christianity for granted forget the birth pangs of the early Church — persecutions that lasted nearly three hundred years. These early followers of Jesus were victorious because of the love they had for Abba and the risen Jesus, and for one another and even for those who hounded them. This kind of enduring, hopeful love was unknown in the pagan world. The pagan world was converted by the joyous, steadfast, hopeful love displayed by Christians under all circumstances. Someone has commented: When Christians lose that love, the world will become pagan once again. Courage is not simply exerting oneself for a moment; it is the ability to face inner chaos and outer difficulty knowing that we are still held in Abba's hand. The ascension of Jesus reminds us that the risen Jesus is cosmically available in every space and time, and that an altar candle burns as brightly as a star.

The best way to finish Paul's Hymn to Love is to look at one who lived the kind of love that Paul wrote about and lived during the time he spread the gospel throughout the ancient world. In 1660, after being imprisoned in England for his religious beliefs, James Naylor was released and reunited with the Society of Friends. Shortly after that he set out from London, intending to visit his wife and children in Wakefield. On the way he was robbed, beaten and left bound in a field. Some members of the Society of Friends found him and brought him into their home where he died. About two hours before he died he spoke the following words, which were taken down as he spoke them:

> There is a spirit which I feel that delights to do no evil, nor to revenge any wrong, but delights to endure all things, in hope to enjoy its own in the end. Its hope is to outlive all wrath and contention, and to weary out all exaltation and cruelty, or whatever is of a nature contrary to itself. It sees to the end of all temptations. As it bears no evil in itself, so it conceives none in thoughts to any other. If it be betrayed, it bears it, for its ground and spring is the mercies and forgiveness of God. Its crown is meekness, its life is ever-

lasting love unfeigned; and takes its kingdom with entreaty and not with contention, and keeps it by lowliness of mind. In God alone it can rejoice, though none else regard it, or can own its life. It's conceived in sorrow, and brought forth without any to pity it, nor doth it murmur at grief and oppression. It never rejoiceth but through sufferings; for with the world's joy it is murdered. I found it alone, being forsaken. I have fellowship therein with them who lived in dens and desolate places in the earth, who through death obtained this resurrection and eternal holy life.

What is love? Love is that divine reality described in Jesus' parables, teaching and life, and in Paul's magnificent summary of the nature of that reality which created the universe and human beings. Love wishes to share with us unconditional caring. We seek that love best when we extend ourselves for the purpose of nurturing our own and another's spiritual, emotional and physical growth and healing. This love can guide us through our crises toward our full human potential. The goal of love is to lead us into the eternal realm, to a place Love has prepared for us. Love is the alpha and omega, the beginning that leads finally to eternal life.

This love can pour through us and we can truly try to be instruments of love. During the dark days in South Africa, a prison chaplain shared with me a description of love that enabled her to continue her seemingly hopeless vocation. In the end, she said, love will conquer whether we are instruments of the Holy One or not. But whether it bears fruit in our broken society depends on us. Love is both fragile and eternally enduring. In the words of Robert Evans and Thomas Parker:

> Love, agape, is the equal and unalterable regard for the value of other human beings independent of their particular characteristics. It extends especially to the helpless and hopeless, to those who have no value in their own eyes and seemingly none for society. Such neighbor-love is costly and sacrificial. It is easily destroyed. In the giver it demands unlimited caring, in the recipient absolute trust.[20]

Who Is My Neighbor?

Jesus used every possible encounter with people to bring them his message that the reign of love was at hand. Love, he proclaimed, has been poured out for us and upon us, and we must direct that love toward all humanity, friend and enemy alike. For example, seventy followers of Jesus had just returned from their mission, amazed because people had welcomed them and because the love which poured through them had healed and given them hope. Jesus in one of his most joyful and hopeful declarations said: "I watched Satan fall from heaven like a flash of lightning." He went on to tell his followers not to rejoice in the amazing things that happened through them, but to rejoice, rather, that their names were written in the heaven of love. Jesus rejoiced that the Holy Spirit was released through them into their broken and agonized world.

Then Jesus took his disciples aside privately and told them how fortunate they were to be seeing evidence of the presence of the kingdom. Just then a scribe, a religious lawyer, broke into their midst. Jesus and his followers fell silent. The scribe asked Jesus a question: "What must I do to inherit eternal life?"

This scribe, however, was not an honest seeker after truth; he was trying to trick Jesus into saying something that could be used against him. But Jesus was not easily caught off guard. He parried with another question: "What is written in the law? How do you read it?" The scribe replied with the summary of the law known to every Jew: "You shall love the Lord your God with all your heart, with all your soul, with all your strength, and with all your mind; and your neighbor as yourself." Jesus nodded his agreement and said, "You have given the right answer; do this and you shall live eternally."

To the scribe, the word "neighbor" included only law-abiding

Jews. In his mind, a Jew need not treat Gentiles, outsiders, law-breakers, tax collectors, prostitutes or Samaritans with kindness. To justify his own position, he asked a second question: "Who is my neighbor?"

Jesus seized this opportunity to teach all who were present — especially his disciples — at the same time that he answered the scribe's question. He did this by telling a story. It is a story that almost everybody knows: the parable of the man beaten by brigands on the road to Jericho and left naked to die in the desert heat. A priest and then a Levite came along, but one after the other they stayed on the other side of the road and passed by. Finally a journeying Samaritan stopped, dressed the man's wounds, and took him on his donkey to Jericho, where he paid for the man's lodging at an inn and took care of him all night long.

Jesus completed his story with a question directed to the scribe: "Who was neighbor to the one who fell among thieves?" The scribe could only give the obvious answer: "The one who showed him mercy." Jesus, looking out over the group that had gathered to hear, said, "Go and do likewise."

One message of this story is quite clear: If we wish to prepare for eternal life, we need to care for those who are lying by the side of the road. We need to reach out to those struck down by life, whether by outer calamity or inner pain and desperation. This message is correct, but several other messages emerge as we reflect on the various characters in Jesus' parable.[1]

Jews and Samaritans

Jesus and his disciples had set out from Galilee to go to Jerusalem for the Passover a few days before Jesus told the story of the Good Samaritan. In order to do so, they had to pass through Samaria. The Jews considered the Samaritans to be apostates and despised them, and the Samaritans returned the compliment. Jews would not walk on the same side of the street with Samaritans. It was a situation we are all familiar with: We often treat those who are closest to us — but who differ with us in small matters — more violently than real enemies.

Jesus and his entourage stopped at a Samaritan town to get some food and spend the night. When the Samaritans turned them away, the disciples were enraged. The fiery James and John, the sons of thunder, screamed out to Jesus: "Lord, shall we call down the fire of heaven to destroy them?" To their chagrin, Jesus scolded them for their attitude: "You have missed the very essence of what I have been trying to teach you. You are to love those who ignore or abuse you. You don't pour vengeance upon them."

A few days after this incident, when Jesus was asked by the scribe, "Who is my neighbor?" he told the story in which a Samaritan, a member of a despised and hated sister religion, is cast in the role of the hero. By means of the story, Jesus was telling both the scribe and his disciples that status or position doesn't count; neither does a grasp of the fine points of religious belief. What counts is that a person reach out — like this outcast Samaritan — with mercy, generosity and love to others in need. Caring actions prepare us for eternal life now and forever. This is kingdom living. Jesus' point was that Samaritans can be closer to the kingdom than those who want vengeance on people who do not welcome them.

His disciples must have smarted when they heard the story. All his Jewish hearers, in fact, would have understood Jesus' message only too clearly. Let us look at each of the characters in the story so that we can understand how we can become true neighbors, like the despised and rejected Samaritan.

The Traveler

First of all, who was this man who went down from Jerusalem to Jericho all alone? Everyone knew that this journey was dangerous. It was simply foolish to go alone; sensible people went in caravans or had an armed guard. Was this man a merchant trying to make a killing by getting to Jericho early? Or was he simply inflated, thinking that no harm could come to him? Perhaps he was ignorant or hard-headed.

No matter. Whoever is dying needs our help, and by giving it we become neighbors, agents of love.

The Bandits

And who were the bandits? Were they ordinary criminals, antisocial people out to mug anyone they could surprise? Since Jesus lived in a foreign-dominated police state, they could also have been political refugees desperate to survive. Like so many anti-government forces, they resorted to the same practices they were trying to overthrow.

Whatever their motives, the robbers took what they wanted and left their victim by the side of the road to die. The sun beat down upon him, and excruciating thirst racked his bleeding body. He was all too conscious, but unable to move.

The Priest

Soon the dying man heard footsteps on the gravel road. Out of the corner of one swollen eye he glimpsed someone coming — a priest. The priest stopped on the opposite side of the road and looked at him. Hope rose in the beaten man's heart. But the priest started walking on again and disappeared down the road.

Passing judgment on the priest is easy, particularly if we don't understand the priest's dilemma. It is so easy for us to be self-righteous. Why didn't the priest stop? According to Jewish law, well known to Jesus' hearers, any priest who touched a dead body must forever forfeit his priesthood — the only position for which he had been prepared, his greatest treasure.

As he looked at the man lying there motionless, the priest feared that the man might die as he was ministering to him. Then he would become unclean and an outcast from his people and his profession. Should he risk everything? His was the noble and ancient task of going into the temple to commune with God and offer sacrifices. Should he jeopardize all that for one unimportant person who probably would die anyway? In addition, nakedness was offensive and unclean. He probably also wondered if the bandits were still nearby.

The Levite

Twenty anguished minutes later the wounded man heard another traveller coming. Hope rekindled. It was a Levite this time. Like the priest, the Levite sized up the situation and decided to keep walking.

Levites were servants in the temple. Like the priests, they gained this privilege by birth. They shared in the glory of the worship of the Most High God. If they touched a corpse, they too were barred from any further service. If they became unclean, they too lost their profession and their position. Like lepers, they became unclean.

Jesus used a priest and a Levite in his story for good reason. He was telling his listeners that when our position or even our religion keeps us from loving care, from reaching out with mercy to those who need us, we fall in step with these two religious leaders who passed by. When we pass by those who need us, we are not living the kingdom of heaven now or preparing for the kingdom of eternity.

In Luke's version of the sermon on the mount, Jesus says some uncomfortable words: "Woe to you who have your consolations and satisfactions and joy now. Woe to you when all speak well of you. Their fathers treated the false prophets in just this way" (Lk 6:24-26). Risking the comforts and security of the good life just to assist a needy person is a very difficult decision to make, but as Jesus declared: "Blessed are the merciful, they shall receive mercy" (Mt 5:7).

The Samaritan

The man was nearly unconscious when the Samaritan happened along. He had nothing to lose; he had no position and was already unclean just by virtue of being a Samaritan. If the bandits were Jews, they wouldn't even have wanted to attack him, since they might be contaminated by touching a Samaritan.

The Samaritan's response was spontaneous. He knew the pain of rejection, and so he was able to reach out and minister to this battered man. His heart was moved with pity, with love, with compassion. If the victim were a Jew and rejected his help, he could bear that too. He would try.

He walked up to the barely conscious man, knelt down by his side, and put his hand gently on the other's head. When the injured man first saw the Samaritan, he was afraid. Would this ancient enemy of his people beat him further or kick his torn body? But now this despised foreigner was giving him a sip of wine. The injured man began to revive. He could hardly believe what was happening to him. Love and compassion from a Samaritan? His stereotype began to crumble.

The Samaritan brought oil and more wine from the bags on his donkey and washed the gaping wounds and bandaged them. He cleaned off the encrusted blood and put a clean garment on the man.

Then, carefully, he raised the man to his feet and helped him sit astride his donkey. He steadied him there and walked beside his beast of burden so that the injured man could lean on his shoulder. They paused whenever they found shade so each could drink more wine and water. Slowly, haltingly, they made the descent to Jericho. At times the rider was so weary and in so much pain that they would stop so that he could lie down to rest. Finally they came to the outskirts of the ancient city.

A shelter for travelers stood near the road. Calling it an inn makes the place sound more glamorous than it was; the place was merely a stable-like building with a section where people could sleep. The Samaritan had stopped there often. He knew the keeper of the caravan stop well and found him. The two of them helped the exhausted, broken man to a cot in a secluded corner. All night long the Samaritan nursed the man until he was certain he would survive; all night long he sat with the stranger. In the morning he called the innkeeper and gave him two silver coins; he had accumulated this amount through many weeks of work. He asked the host to take care of him. If his care cost more than what he had paid, he would make up the difference when he came that way again. Then he laid his hand upon the shoulder of the man who had fallen among thieves, blessed him, and went on his way.

Becoming a Neighbor

How did the Samaritan become such a genuinely loving person? How can we become more like him, a neighbor as he was a neighbor?

The Samaritan believed that reaching out with genuine concern to others in distress was a most important task. As a Samaritan, his Bible contained only the first five books of our Bible, but this was enough to give him a glimpse of the God of love. He had read the story of Joseph who forgave the very brothers who sold him into slavery. He believed that God was a loving God, a caring God, and that love and caring were therefore part of the very fabric of the universe. In his own times of suffering, he had turned to this benevolent God and received compassion.

Instead of wishing to wreak vengeance on his enemies, he wanted to give others the same kind of mercy that he had received when he turned to the Creator in his own folly, bitterness, sinfulness, and anguish. Because he lived among people who despised him, he knew that if he did not respect and love himself as God loved him, he probably would not survive and would not be able to care for people who hated him.

He knew that he could never love others, and keep his soul from the damage that persecution frequently causes, unless he paused often in the mysterious, loving light of God, and accepted himself as God did. He had discovered through experience that when he felt rejected and despised, it was nearly impossible to maintain a proper view of himself unless he could stop and rest in the tender, gracious, eternal love of the Creator.

A Neighbor to Ourselves

We are discovering today that if we do not accept ourselves, we cannot accept others. If we think our own faults are so horrible that we must bury them deep in our unconscious, we likely will see, condemn, and punish them in others. Learning to be good Samaritans to ourselves is essential to becoming good Samaritans to others. To accept ourselves in our wretchedness is one of the most difficult tasks in life. But as we do so, we are able to reach out and love others in all their wretchedness.

The psychiatrist C. G. Jung has written that even doctors have trouble accepting people who pour out the ugly and distorted aspects of their lives. He then went on to say that none of us feels truly accepted until the worst in us is accepted too. If we wish to be of help to others or accompany them a step on the way, we must be in touch with the depth of the others' souls. We are never in touch with them when we pass judgment.[2]

Nearly all the saints agree with Paul's cry in Romans 7:24, "Wretched man that I am! Who will rescue me from this body of death?" But few have expressed this need for self-honesty better than Catherine of Siena; she believed that there could be no fire of deep loving without the wood of self-knowing. To her confessor she wrote: "I would have you never cease increasing the fuel for the fire of holy desire, the wood of self-knowledge. This is the wood that nourishes and feeds the fire of divine love; this love is acquired by the knowledge of self and of the inestimable love of God. . . . The more fuel one gives to the fire, so much the more increases the warmth of love of Christ and neighbor. So remain hidden in the knowledge of self."[3]

Able to face himself in the presence of God, the Samaritan no longer judged others. All true neighbors learn to follow this path of self-acceptance and caring.

After the Samaritan was sure that his charge would recover, he went upon his way. He did not hang onto the injured man. He would be available if he were needed, but he did not cling — he did not use his neighborliness to meet his own needs. Sometimes needy ones to whom we have been neighbors become our closest friends, but this kind of relationship needs to be initiated by the other and always remain mutual.

Whenever I meditate on the story of the man who fell among thieves and the despised Samaritan who saved him, I see again the incredible depth of Jesus' parables. I realize anew what I need to do to become a neighbor to those who need me most. I realize that unless I believe that love springs from the core of the universe, I will seldom make it a first priority to work hard at loving others. When I lack this belief, I am out of synch with the center of reality and lose touch with it.

I need to look honestly and deeply at myself and love this person I am, with my innumerable faults, because Christ died for me and would have died for me if I had been the only person on earth. Then I need to let God's love flow through me out to the neighbor that God places in my path.[4]

So Many Neighbors

Facing the enormous number of people around us who would like to share our love can be overwhelming. There are so many needy people in the world. As we become more aware of them, they begin to knock at our doors. A visitor to India, after several days in the slums there, said to Mother Teresa of Calcutta: "How do you stand it? Here you are in this enormous city. You work continually and do not touch more than one percent of the suffering and dying in Calcutta." Mother Teresa answered, "I was not called to be successful; I was only called to be faithful."

All we can do is to be faithful. In a global world we are in touch with a staggering number of suffering neighbors. We have already noted that before we set out to change the world, we need to take time to be quiet and to reflect on what the God of love wishes us to become. Love does not want to destroy us, but rather to enlist us as instruments of love. When Francis of Assisi was dying, he was asked if he would have changed anything in his ministry. He responded: "I would have been more kind to my body." If we do not stay within our limits, we will become another burden for others. After we have basked in the loving presence of the risen Christ, we need to list our priorities. We have many places we can share ourselves, and it is important to prioritize them. In the next chapter I will suggest some ideas about how we can prepare to love our very different neighbors. For now, though, I must stress that until we take time out to set priorities, life will run us, and we will not be able to give our best to ourselves or to our neighbors.

Neighbors to Consider

Human beings are social beings. I have already mentioned the many infants who have died in nursing homes; they were not picked up, held, and enjoyed, and they simply died. Babies who have survived without any human contact are hardly human. Interaction and contact with others are essential to emotional and intellectual development; language itself is something we only learn through hearing our parents and friends talk to us, and we teach other children as we play with them.

The family unit is the place where we become capable of love. In many cultures, infants are carried with their mothers in a sling close to the mother's body — even when she is working in the field. And the home is the cradle not only of love but also of faith, hope, and courage, of life and growth. Some studies indicate that even the physical height that growing children attain is related to the amount of love they have received. But of course families can also be places of tensions and frustration, pain, neglect, physical abuse, and sarcasm. We need to reflect on the question:

How can we make our homes places of creative, nurturing love? A loving atmosphere seldom exists unless parents have made a priority of providing such an environment. Growing up in a real home himself, Jesus assumed that we would try our best to provide such homes.

As adults, we need friends beyond the family, men and women with whom we can relate as peers. We need spiritual companions, people with whom we can share our spiritual life, our social life, our athletic interests, our artistic gifts. However, these relationships are self-defeating if they take precedence over our families, our parents, our children, and our grandchildren.

We also are in touch with a vast group of people whom we meet at work, at church, or at the Parent Teacher Association (PTA). We meet other people as employers or employees. When our children are young, we can be involved with other parents in their activities. One of the great opportunities for churches is to provide groups with social and religious goals for all ages. James Lynch in his book *The Broken Heart* shows that most adults who have no social contacts begin to deteriorate. His studies show that these people are more prone to fatal heart attacks; he gives evidence that people who go to church once a week and sit next to a warm body are less likely to have heart problems. *We really need each other.*

As loving people we need to be open not only to family and friends but also to strangers. Have you ever been a stranger in a new town or in a foreign land? In ancient Greek culture, being banished from the homeland was considered as severe as the death penalty; being a stranger in a strange land was intolerable. In years of pastoring three different churches, one of my least successful tasks was enabling the congregation to greet and welcome strangers. It is ironic that this would be a problem in churches, of all places, since Jesus said, "When you welcome strangers, you are welcoming me."

Jesus was also very clear about loving our enemies. He gave us little credit for loving our friends or families; even the pagans and tax collectors do that. But how do we go about loving our enemies? This takes great discipline and love (Mt 5:43-47). We will have much more to say on this subject.

Few people need companionship more than the sick. A short visit and a prayer are like the balm of Gilead to them. The elderly sick, furthermore, are often alone and unable to get adequate food. A pot of hot soup tastes like ambrosia to the lonely. Elderly and sick people are often placed in what are euphemistically called "rest homes." Many times all of their generation have passed away, and their families simply can't be bothered to care for them or visit. They become prisoners unable to decide their own fates; they live shadow lives often forgotten by their own. Any friendly visit gives them great joy.

Although modern prisons were developed to avoid the brutal punishment that was formerly meted out to those who broke away from law and custom, prisons remain profoundly lonely places. I have visited many in prisons, and I have corresponded with many prisoners. In few places have I received more gratitude. Jesus also reminded us that when we are visiting prisoners, we are visiting him — and he added no qualification in regard to what the person has done. Most prisons are schools of crime, not places where people can be healed. This is partly because too few of us have followed Christ into a prison to visit one of the least of his brothers and sisters.

In recent years we have come to see that the dying need love right up to death and that the sorrowing family needs continued love as they deal with grief. In fact, however, the dying are often abandoned, though most of them long to have a caring person with them as they step into a new dimension of reality. Great grief in my own life opened me to the pain and loss that come to many as they slip into death. For four months I traveled each week through ice and snow to visit my mother as she died. Her gratitude was boundless. But I myself was grieving, and I wish that there had been, at that time, some wise and caring person who had reached out to me with understanding and love. Another vivid experience of sharing God's consolation came to me in my first parish. I discovered and visited a homeless woman who was actually dying in an abandoned railroad station. Her eyes brightened each time I stepped through the door. I came often, and I was the only person at the funeral that I held for her. When we minister to the dying, we can have no expectation of receiving anything in return. It is pure gift.

Those who suffer from depression and discouragement are usually unable to reach out to anyone. They become strangers and foreigners in their own land. Because many of us are afraid of our own darkness, we are afraid to reach out to those who need us; even if we cannot help, however, we can at least find someone who can. But if we are in touch with our own darkness, we can often aid our depressed neighbors. One day, for example, a gifted but depressed young man came into my office at the University of Notre Dame. I listened as he talked, and then I was able to say, "Yes, I know what the darkness is like. I have been there." He was no longer alone, and we became friends; he recovered and became a psychotherapist and has written an excellent book, *Beyond Depression.*[5] Later Andy Canale was able to be with our son when he was facing darkness and death.

Often church people avoid discussing religion with those who call themselves atheists or agnostic. Are we not sure enough of our ground? Are we not secure in our own beliefs? These ungrounded people need us; they too are our neighbors. We need to remember, though, that few can be changed by argument. Constant unjudging concern and love are the best key to opening a heart closed by an uncaring society. The early Church never would have grown had it not reached out to cynical pagans. Love often softens desperate intellectual meaninglessness. It may be the only force that can.

The first free homes for the sick and broken in the history of civilization were built and maintained by the early Christians. The pagan world viewed those stricken with sickness and disaster as people struck down by the gods and goddesses. The emperor Julian (who during the fourth century tried to bring the Roman Empire back to paganism) wrote: "Now we can see what makes Christians such powerful enemies of our gods. It is the brotherly love which they manifest toward strangers and toward the sick and the poor."[6] No Christian statement could substantiate the vitality of Christian loving outreach as well as these words by Christianity's enemy. Whether by prayer or medical means, healing is one aspect of love shared with neighbors.

Reaching out to the poor, the homeless and disadvantaged is another way we can be called to express our love. Remember the situation of the men and women first attracted to the Christian fellowship: They were displaced people. The Church of the Savior in Washington, D.C., is one of the finest examples of this kind of outreach I know. In addition to providing the finest ministry to hurting and homeless people in the slums of Washington, it provides teaching and training for those who find themselves called to this expression of Christian love.

The founder of The Church of the Savior, Gordon Cosby, was a chaplain during the Normandy invasion in 1944. During one of the first engagements, the two other chaplains were killed. Cosby knew he could not possibly minister alone to all the anguish of the sick and dying, of those who had lost companions, and of those who faced death daily. Out of prayer came the solution. He picked those who seemed interested in and capable of ministering; he trained them. During the fierce fighting, his battalion was reduced from three thousand to sixteen hundred soldiers, but the soldiers maintained hope because each person had a spiritual leader to turn to. In the Church of the Savior, Cosby used the same method of teaching lay people to minister to the sickness, poverty, and agony of slum life, and also to provide the spiritual life that alone can keep the love of servant and leader alive and strong.[7]

People like William Wilberforce have been called to serve in still another way: by changing the inhuman structures of society that destroy human beings. We live in a world where many people have no opportunity to develop to the maximum of their potential. The finest book dealing with this enormous subject is by Walter Wink: *Engaging the Powers, Discernment and Resistance in a World of Domination*. This book is the summation of a life dedicated to the study of this aspect of love.[8]

As I look over these pages, I realize that several needs take top priority. I need first of all to stay in touch with the source of love and to allow myself to be loved so I can genuinely give love to others. Then I need to share love with those with whom I am most closely associated, my family, my friends, the ones with whom I work. When I am confronted by the beaten person (whether physically or psychologically wounded), I need to give whatever assistance I can and then bring that person to someone else who can care for him or her. I cannot reach out personally to all those whose need touches me. But I can pray. Intercessory prayer is a real ministry of love — especially for those confined to their home. And I can call people on the phone, as well as write and answer letters.

The incomparable paintings of Vincent Van Gogh depict his vision of a world filled with divine light; but without the letters Vincent wrote and that his brother Theo answered, Van Gogh might not have lived to create those paintings. We never know the final effect of a kind, spoken word, or of a letter inspired by deep loving concern. Without expression, our love may never touch one who needs it.

Those who cannot go out into the world can share money to enable others to work in their stead. Remember the praise Jesus gave to the widow who gave part of her substance in the temple. Giving money is a form of love.

In quiet before God we need to listen deeply and then decide in what way we are called to be channels of the Holy One's unconditional love to the world. As I write these words, I believe that my task at present is to use the written word to share what I have learned in the last thirty years since my experience on that airplane. In addition, my family and friends, or my own quiet time with the Other, cannot be neglected. Many minsters (lay and clerical) have burned out when they have not kept in touch with the source of love. What we do for ego reasons will eventually burn us out; what we do as instruments of love strengthens us and fills us more.

We have been looking at the positive effects of love. Let us look at the destructive effects of *not* loving where our love was really needed and we were responsible for giving it.

The Sole Treason

The only real betrayal of life is the refusal to love, for it is this refusal that gives evil a chance to grow. When we refuse to give first place to love, which unites and draws our lives together into wholeness, evil in its true form of separation and disintegration is given a foothold in our own lives. We often try to find excuses not to love, to see reasons which give us a right not to love, particularly when the person who needs our love is one who embarrasses us or seems unlovable. In this way we have given evil a chance to germinate and grow in the one place we can affirm life — in ourselves and those around us. In *The Seed and the Sower*, Laurens Van der Post tells a story of just such a betrayal of life, told in so moving a way that it brought tears to my eyes. The wonder of his story, however, lies in the fact (based on an actual occurrence) that the betrayal was recognized and redeemed by a concrete action of love — before it was too late.

At a conference I took a walk with Bruno Klopfer, a superb counselor and the leading authority on the Rorschach or "ink blot" test. We were talking about the unbelievable healing effects of simple loving outreach to other people. He told me this story: One of his students was given the assignment to administer an experimental Rorschach to a woman who had been institutionalized in a Colorado state hospital for five years. She had had both electro-shock and insulin shock therapy, and her condition had finally been judged incurable. But the Rorschach showed some signs of life. Because the student had had no training in psychotherapy, Dr. Klopfer purposely selected him and suggested that he return to see the woman once a week, just for a friendly visit. He saw her six times, and after the sixth visit the woman was well enough to return home. In commenting on the story, Dr. Klopfer stated that fifty percent of all psychotherapy is essentially the effect of loving concern, nothing more than genuine interest in another human being— something which certainly need not be limited to the psychiatrist's office.

Why is it so hard for us to love one another, even members of our own families? We let our pride and hurt, our angers and buried grudges bubble up and batter other people. Then we look around our world at the feuds among nations that go back for five hundred years or more, and at the senseless violence in many of our societies; we fail to realize that all this hatred is really a reflection of the dark side that exists in all of us. When we do not see our own violence and ferocity, we have little chance to keep them in check. When G. K. Chesterton was asked what was wrong with the world, he wrote: "Dear Sirs, I am. Sincerely Yours, G. K. Chesterton."

Biological impulses lie beneath humanity's fierce activities. Built into our very bodies is the instinct for survival — no matter who suffers. (No wonder people viewed the willing martyrdom of the early Christians with such amazement; martyrdom seems biologically unnatural.) Under attack, our sympathetic nervous system prepares us for either fight or flight, for attack or withdrawal. At adolescence, testosterone begins to flow in young men, and they become more aggressive and violent; indeed, studies of young offenders in jail show that these people often have a highly increased level of this male hormone.

If we believe that we live in a purely material universe, then we assume that human nature amounts to nothing more than this biology. There is no place for good or evil; the universe is value-free. Within this mechanistic framework, what gives a person the most power to indulge in the most pleasure becomes the only criterion for human behavior. No truly satisfactory system of morality has ever been devised within a meaningless, materialistic universe. The only power that can tame our fierce destructiveness is the experience of love from other human beings and the conviction that our universe was created by love and that divine Love still seeks us out to bring harmony to us and to our troubled world.

Without love, human life either withers away and falls into the abyss or turns to violence and destruction. If children are not genuinely loved, they do not mature properly, do not learn, do not even grow; when children are not a part of truly loving families, they are likely to become members of violent gangs. In *The Face Beside the Fire,* Van der Post describes a poison we give to those close to us, families or friends, if we do not love them. Those who do not receive love at home, where it might reasonably have been expected, are not merely let down in a neutral limbo; they can actually be destroyed. Van der Post writes of a woman and the husband she had ceased to love: "Slowly she is poisoning Albert. . . . This poison . . . is found in no chemist's book. . . . It is a poison brewed from all the words, the delicate, tender, burning trivialities and petty endearments she's never used — but would so constantly have spoken if she'd truly loved him."[9] This statement is even more true of children.

Those who have never been loved seldom have a sense of real worth or value, of security or permanence, for it is only when we are loved that we can begin to treat ourselves as human. Deep in the heart of each of us is the fear that no one can abide us. This is the result of our separation from God, and only as the human soul is watered with concern and love can this disfigurement within it be cleansed away and replaced by a new growth of security and self-respect.

Faith, Courage and Hope

Faith is also a product of love, and one who has never been loved seldom has faith. How can we believe that there is a God who cares and watches over us until we learn this love from some human being and thus are given a glimmering realization of the nature of that love which dwells at the core of reality?

Courage is another result of having been loved. The really fearful, really frightened men and women who lack courage to go out and take on life are simply individuals who have never known love. These fearful ones have never known what it is to have another person standing by them, encouraging and loving them. Courage is manifest in the actions of those who have confidence in the ultimate nature of reality; they can step out to risk the present for their future, the proximate for the ultimate. They arrive at this point by accepting the confidence and trust that spring from being loved. It is practically impossible to be truly courageous unless we have known the healing balm, the psychic stuff which is love. How can we go through the dark night of the soul, through which courage often leads, unless first we are grounded in love?

Nor is it possible to have hope without having known the reality of love. Love gives meaning. How can we hope for good in the future, the greatest gift, unless we have known something of it in the past? Without love there is nothing to look forward to, nothing to imagine as the fulfillment of life, and so there is no hope.

Strange, isn't it, that God would put into our human hands such a tremendous power? By loving or not loving we can create or destroy, build up or tear down. How audacious God was to put in our hands the lives of those around us, and our lives in their hands. What faith God has in us.

If we love, we create, heal, release in those around us a power that seldom fails. If we do not love, we join the forces of the evil one and destroy as effectively as if we were triggering a machine gun into a defenseless crowd. If we love, we step into the circle of the very creative life of God. If we do not love, do not in our hearts go out in compassion and show love in action, then we step into the down-draft of evil which is destroying the world we live in. What a terrible responsibility God and life have put into our hands.

When we have not been loved, it is very difficult to learn to love, but not impossible. Van der Post reminds us that the inability to love is a far greater tragedy: "For do we not all know, in our aboriginal hearts, that the tragedy of the individual is not so much not being loved as being unable to love, as if by some dark impediment which seems to cut us off from the full rhythm of

Life?"[10] Our loving keeps us from contributing to this kind of tragedy.

We can either become fonts of creativity and life, or, by not loving, cauldrons of witches' brew, poisoning the lives of all we touch. It is not even a simple question of *what we do*, but in the long run a question of *how we do it*. After all, Satan's real fault in the old story was that he wanted to do things more rationally and efficiently than he could by continuing in the life and way of God's love.

So our task as Christians and all seekers, as women and men truly trying to be in touch with ultimate reality, is learning to love. What we need to pass on is not so much information about the Old or New Testaments, about proper beliefs, but the real experience of actual love. Should not any Christian community, and our community in particular, be a place in which just such understanding, consolation, and love are given and received, in which each of us grows deeper and deeper in our experience of these realities? The really vital churches are those that provide fellowship in which real love grows.

Growth in love is possible if we see how important it is and are willing to put our best effort into following Jesus more fully. If this is so, then we need to turn to some very practical questions about how we can begin to show more love, more of the spirit of which Jesus spoke.

Silence, Love and Prayer

The fruit of silence is prayer.
The fruit of prayer is faith.
The fruit of faith is LOVE.
The fruit of love is service.
The fruit of service is peace.

Mother Teresa[1]

Genuine religious love begins with silence. The Holy One will occasionally break through to us even when we are active, as the risen Jesus did to Paul on the Damascus road. However, before Paul could effectively present the good news of divine unconditional love for all human beings, he had to retire to the silence of the desert for many years. He learned that prayer is not so much asking for things, petition, as it is communion with the Divine — knowing and accepting God's love for us. Paul came *to know* the reality that totally remade him: His faith became secure.[2] In the desert Paul encountered a reality that lifted him out of himself and gave him extraordinary revelations. This experience gave him the conviction and faith that sustained him through his trials and tribulations. He also learned that his actions toward others and all of his gifts must be directed by and in the service of the love he had encountered.

Paul, the persecutor of the Christians, was totally changed. From his love came his faithful service in founding new Christian communities. His continued service gave him a sense of inner peace. When he was taken to prison in Rome, he did not know which was more important, to die and be with Christ or to stay and work with the Churches. In that peace that came with service, he could return to silence and again know unconditional love;

108

then he was able to go out and continue his loving service. Paul continued on his spiral pathway, alternating times of silence and times of action, until he was martyred in Rome.

The Mystery of Silence

All the great religions of humankind remind us that we human beings are not able to attain our full religious potential until we have learned to be silent. Most great literature, poetry, art and music spring out of silence. The solitary Austrian novelist and poet, Franz Kafka, shared the secret of his creativity in these words:

> You need not leave your room. Remain sitting at your table and listen. You need not even listen, simply wait. You need not even wait, just learn to become quiet, and still, and solitary. The world will freely offer itself to you to be unmasked. It has no choice; it will roll in ecstasy at your feet.[3]

In *Sartor Resartus*, Thomas Carlyle expressed the same view in his characteristically rugged style. Few religious statements have touched me, stung me, and stayed with me more than these words that I first read sixty years ago:

> Silence and Secrecy! Altars might still be raised to them (were this an altar-building time) for universal worship. Silence is the element in which great things fashion themselves together, that at length they may emerge, full-formed and majestic, into the daylight of life, which they are thenceforth to rule.... Nay, in thy own mean perplexities, do thou thyself but *hold thy tongue for one day*: on the morrow, how much clearer are thy purposes and duties; what wreck and rubbish have those mute workmen within thee swept away, when intrusive noises were shut out! ... As the Swiss inscription says: *Sprechen ist silbern, Schweigen ist golden* (Speech is silver, Silence is golden); or as I might rather express it: Speech is of Time, Silence is of Eternity.[4]

The prophets of Israel and the psalmist speak of the need for silence in order to listen to Jahweh. Jesus similarly left his busy ministry among hordes of people seeking hope and healing to go by himself into the lonely hills of Galilee. If Jesus needed time alone with Abba before he continued his ministry of preaching and healing, certainly I require it even more. The great monastic groups, both Orthodox and Catholic, lived silence and taught silence. But few ordinary people of our time have understood the necessity of silence in order to experience the Holy One and then to share divine love with the hungry people around them. About a century ago Kierkegaard reminded his readers that a real Christian

> . . . often feels a need of solitude, which for him is a vital necessity — sometimes like breathing, at other times like sleeping. The fact that he feels this vital necessity more than other men is also a sign that he has a deeper nature. Generally the need of solitude is a sign that there is spirit in a man after all, and it is a measure for what spirit there is.[5]

If the practice of silence was difficult in Kierkegaard's time, it is much more difficult in our own. We spend much of modern life in a studied attempt to avoid ever being alone, to avoid being faced with the full reality of the depth within us. The media have invaded nearly every moment of our lives. Waking by a radio alarm clock, we hear some quiet music and then are bombarded with the latest tragedies in our world or the latest gyrations of the financial markets. Then comes breakfast with spouse or children, with the newspaper before our eyes and more T.V. in the background. If both parents are going to work and there are children, the mad rush to get everyone on their way occurs each weekday. If a parent is home with small children, that person experiences a busyness that is only understandable to those who have been through it: One expert on prayer told me as we were discussing prayer that the only person with a real excuse for having no time for silence or prayer is a woman with several small children.

If we drive to work, we are likely to be joined to the radio again; if we take a train or bus to work, we encounter the hubbub of other passengers. Even at work itself we are often accompanied by pipeline music. Most lunches are sacred business appointments or conversations. Then the noise of radios and traffic accompanies us home, followed by concentration on something to eat. Few families have real communication; often T.V. dinners are eaten before the tube. Then comes serious T.V. or a meeting or a video, after which we fall into bed, too tired to dream. When we can't sleep, we have a sleeping pill near at hand to ensure that there will be no nighttime encounter with silence. And each day is another boring repetition of the day before.

How To Be Silent

Reaching out beyond ourselves in genuine love is nearly impossible until we are silent. The first step in achieving silence is stopping our own talking, obvious as that may seem. We shall show later on that any real listening (so central to love) is likewise impossible until we stop talking. One of Charles Williams' finest novels, *All Hallows Eve*, is the story of a woman (it could just as well have been a man) who denies herself entrance into heaven simply because she is always talking and never hears the instructions on how to arrive at that destination.

The next step is again obvious. We need to make a conscious decision to learn how to be silent. We need to make the effort to find out if we can receive something in silence and on the other side of silence. Busyness is not *of* the devil; it *is* the devil. But going against the cultural norm is always difficult; our families may look askance at us when we suggest that we need some time alone to be silent. Learning to be silent requires discipline — even more discipline than that required for learning to play a violin.[6]

The third thing we need to do is to set aside time for being quiet. We need to use our best time, day or night, for being silent. We are then free to reflect on all aspects of ourselves. For some people the best time for silence is in the morning, while for others the best time is in the middle of the day. Some people like a period of quiet just before they retire. And then there are some who wake up in the middle of the night. These times may change in different phases of our lives.

None of us has perfect memories. Even if what we experience is of great importance, we can easily forget what we have not written down. Great experiences of compassion can slip away into the haze of forgetfulness; actions where we have been un-kind or thoughtless can lie hidden and uncorrected if we do not find a way to keep from forgetting them. Remembering the complexities of our lives and our relationships to other human beings and to God is nearly impossible unless we keep some *written* record of our lives. Of course, not everyone will need to keep a written record. The saintly Brother Lawrence, for instance, could neither read nor write, but he tried to perform every act, from serving a meal to picking up a straw from the floor, as a service to God. His whole being expressed his love and praise of God and his love for others, and people of all stages of life came from all over Europe to learn from this scullery cook. But most of us who are sincerely seeking to grow in love of God and human beings can read and write, and we can profit greatly by keeping some record of our progress on our spiritual journey.

Silence can lead us directly into the divine presence. Some experience this as a sense of holy presence; some are offered an image that is luminous with meaning. Other people speak of a dazzling darkness. There are some who hear a still, small voice. Great numbers of people feel lifted out of themselves and charged with new energy and life by these experiences.[7] We can easily forget these experiences, however, unless we record them in some way — either writing them, typing them into our com-puter, or speaking them into a tape recorder. The remembrance that the Holy One loves us unconditionally is one of the most difficult experiences to retain. We also have a tendency to forget insights about our failures in love and in listening to others; we forget our angry or harsh words, our neglect of those close to us. When we read over what we have written, we are reminded of our imperfections and our need to work on them and to seek God's help in loving. When we write down the times we have missed the mark of caring for others, we are more likely to change.[8]

We need a place where we can disappear and be quiet and where we will not be disturbed. One friend kept a time for quiet in the morning after her husband and children had left home. If the phone rang, she would answer it and say: "I have someone with me. May I call you back?" Also, the ringer on most phones can be turned off. Those with answering machines can let the machine take the message. Only the most adept religious person can be quiet in the midst of confusion and noise.

Once we have secured a place of quiet, we need to find a physical position in which we are alert and comfortable. Each of us needs to find which position fits us best. The first position in yoga is simply to lie prone on one's back with arms and legs stretched out. Some of us can be quiet sitting in a comfortable chair.

If we are to be really quiet and still, we must stop all outer activity. It is true that one kind of prayer can be carried on while washing the dishes or working in the garden; however, total listening to the depth of ourselves and hearing the voice of love require our total attention.

Having stopped all our outer activity, we should then try to stop our inner thoughts and desires, the movements of mind and will. This is more difficult. Sometimes saying a simple phrase like "Jesus, mercy" or the Jesus Prayer ("Lord Jesus Christ, Son of God, have mercy on me, a sinner") can help us settle down. Roman Catholics may find the "Hail Mary" useful. Another help is to stop my inner talking, quietly ceasing to talk to myself. When talking to myself, I find that the muscles around my voice box move slightly; I am not totally still physically when I am talking to myself. One person reported that the hum of her vacuum cleaner gave her a sense of total quiet and left her in a meditative state. Watching a lighted candle can also help some of us.

As I become still, I begin to think of the things I have left undone, the calls I should have made, the letters I should have written, the jobs I need to do. Sometimes ideas for my writing come to me, or I think of people I need to phone. I find it helpful to have my journal at hand so I can write these things down and tell myself that I will take care of them later. If I try to hold onto these ideas and yet be still, I effectively destroy any real possibility of becoming truly quiet within. I find, therefore, that sitting quietly with pencil in hand and with a journal before me focuses my attention and opens me to silence. My wife, however, finds that this practice puts a total stop to any meaningful quiet or meditation; only after she has finished her quiet does she record her insights. So we each need to find our own way.

I often get up when I awaken in the middle of the night for my time of holy silence. At that time I am already quiet, so I do not have to spend time getting quiet. The phone seldom rings. My wife is in bed sleeping. When we had our children with us, they also were in bed and quiet.

As long as my mind is raging with thoughts, ideas, plans, and fears about the physical world, I cannot listen significantly to God or any other dimension of reality. In his book, *The Doors of Perception*, Aldous Huxley suggested that our sense organs, nervous systems, and brains are basically eliminative in nature. They are designed to help us survive on the surface of this particular planet, and so they cut down or tune out many other possible realms of experience. They rivet our attention on the physical realm and keep us from being confused and overwhelmed by much useless and irrelevant information. However, in the process of doing this they keep us out of touch with other dimensions of reality, the spiritual dimensions that humans can experience in addition to the physical one. In quietness we find detachment and so untie ourselves from total attention to outer, physical reality. Then we sometimes find another kind of experience breaking through. Only those entirely brainwashed by Western materialism will ignore this possibility.[9]

Becoming truly silent cannot be done in a hurry; it is a slow, deliberate process like eating an artichoke. One enjoys this giant thistle, leaf by leaf. Finally we come to the delicious heart of the artichoke. If one tries to eat it in any other way, one ends with a mouthful of spines. The heart of silence is infinitely more delicious than an artichoke, but reaching it requires the same kind of patience.

As I begin to be still, I may well become aware of tension in many parts of my body. When I am tense, I am not quiet. Tension is preparation for action, being on guard. Tension is congealed action. Often I may not even realize that I am as taut as a rubber band until I take the time to be still. I can then quietly let go of tension, starting with the top of my head, moving over my face, down my neck, down my arms, down my torso to my legs. This is only necessary when I discover tension within me. Most of us, however, have some tension most of the time; and this exercise is a good one for all of us from time to time — for physical reasons as well as for coming to religious silence.

Most Eastern religions speak of the importance of breathing when we are trying to be quiet. I cannot be still when I am huffing and puffing like a steam engine. Breathing is the only major bodily function which can be controlled both consciously and unconsciously. Slowing down breathing to seven or eight breaths a minute has a quieting effect on the whole body. Classical Christian writers like the Greek fathers on Mount Athos and Ignatius of Loyola recommended deep and quiet breathing as an aid to quieting down and meditating, or even as an aid to praying the Lord's Prayer.

Sometimes when people try to become quiet, they fall asleep. If it happens only occasionally, this may indicate insufficient rest, and we should enjoy it and get more sleep. We might even have a helpful dream. If sleep happens often, however, we can try various practices to stay awake in our quiet time. The main caution is not to get angry or upset about going to sleep, or we will be lifted right out of our silence.

One of the reasons for recording dreams is that they spring naturally out of the quietness of sleep and reveal another dimension of reality. In deep quiet, dreamlike images and pictures may begin to bubble up out of the depths of the soul. When this occurs, we have entered consciously into the realm of the soul from which dreams emerge. Together with alpha brain waves, such images are a sign that we are truly quiet. We can turn inward and watch these images flow by us and become imageless peace. However, another kind of meditation involves following these images and trying to understand them and their meaning. Dream images were often considered messengers of the divine in the Bible, among the Church Fathers and even up to the present time in Greek Orthodox Churches. The great nineteenth-century educator, John Bosco, was led by his amazing dreams, and his Pope instructed him to keep a record of them.[10]

Many people find that being quiet with others helps them quiet down and become silent. An atmosphere of quiet engenders quiet. We cannot always depend on others for coming into quietness, but periods of quietness with others in a prayer group can help us establish an atmosphere in which we come to an inner calm. Entering into the quiet of a eucharistic celebration can also bring us to a deep sense of the love and presence of the risen Christ. In the family intimacy and silence of an early-morning service of eucharist, we can know this love in a concrete way that brings us to the cleansing and healing love of Christ. One of the main purposes of the great mystery of eucharist is to bring us into the presence of unconditional love — love that is mentioned on nearly every page of the full Catholic missal.

As we conclude our daily time of quiet and listening, we need to take three or four minutes to move back into the busy and confusing outer world. Meditating in the middle of the night has one advantage; we do not need this threshold time to be quiet, and when we finish, we can simply return to the deeper restfulness of sleep. After our quiet time it is helpful to record any new images or insights before we go back into the busyness of ordinary life.

A Personal Encounter within the Silence

Once I was complaining to a wise friend that I often awakened at about two o'clock in the morning and then could not get back to sleep. The friend asked me if I really wanted to know why I awoke. I did want to know, for the days after these sleepless nights were a grim ordeal. So he told me that God wanted to talk with me. With my watered-down liberal theological training, I thought he was making fun of me, and I said so. He replied sincerely: "God woke up Samuel in order to talk to him. Why do you think that the Holy One won't speak to you in your darkness? Do you think that God has changed?"

Since I had found that the Divine had directed me out of a dead-end street through my dreams, I thought that listening for God in a sleepless night might well be worth a try. The following night when I awoke, I got up and went to a place where I could be warm. With journal and pencil in hand, I spoke inwardly: "Well, God, here I am, what do you have on your mind?" To my utter amazement, something spoke back to me. I recorded both the questions and the answers. A real conversation followed, and these conversations have continued many nights during the past forty years.

Each nighttime conversation is different, but they are all variations on one theme. Out of them have come great clarity in seeing what is amiss within me and an impetus toward change within my life. In them I have been moved to efforts of restitution, forgiveness, and love. From these times of nightly dialogue I have come to know that there is an Other who wishes to lead me and guide me. This Other loves me beyond my wildest imagination. This is the Spirit of love and wisdom, Hagia Sophia. Anything of value that has come to me or through me has come from this source. Most important, I find that each of us has infinite value and worth, in spite of everything we do to mar or spoil our essential and infinite value. Here is the first of these written dialogues:

Well, Lord, here I am. A friend told me that I should come here in the middle of the night and ask you what you have on your mind. Are you there? Do you wish to talk with me? You know that I need my sleep.

I want you, my child, and want to help you become what you are capable of becoming. I love you and want to give you that love.

Why don't you do it at a more reasonable time, during the day or in the evening?

I can never get your attention then. You are so busy that if I am to break through with love and concern for you I must make you uncomfortable and get to you in the middle of the night when you wouldn't think of doing anything else.

If it hadn't been for Max Zeller, I would never have understood the message of my sleeplessness. I might have gone down the drain. That hardly seems like kindness and concern.

Just because you have forgotten how to listen to the depth is no reason that I am not who I am. It is not really my fault that you have not heard the message of scripture and the Church. I am always here and seeking your fellowship. You have been so caught up with the outer world and your own ideas that you have forgotten the reality of the inner world.

Why do you want me? I am of no value. You must know all my faults and lusts and angers. How could you love me?

Child, child, how little you understand. I am love. I can no more help loving you and all human beings than the leopard can change his spots. It is my nature to love, and I have created all human beings because I wanted to love them and have them respond to me. I long for them to stop and receive my love.

You mean that you can care for me? Me, with all my stupidity, anger, self-will, egotism?

That is the whole point of my being. I would have died for you if you had been the only human being. It is your very need for me which makes my love flow even more. Those who are getting along well don't need my love as much as those who are lost and struggling and in pain.

If you really care for me and if you are really there, I don't have to do it all on my own. I don't have to be afraid.

That is right, but before this day is over, you will forget this conversation, this encounter, and chalk it up to illusion. You will get busy and forget.

What then would you have me do?

Have the courage to come back each night that you awaken and get restored. Have the discipline to get up and talk with me even if you lose your sleep. Then during the day pause and remember that I am with you and will help you through the day. Seek me before you make any decisions or take important actions. Remember that I am here and I love you and that since I have conquered even death, you don't have to fear anything, even death.

I'll try to come back and I will try to remember. Help me, Lord.

We are all very different. Each of us will find that the Spirit of God will touch us according to our needs, in terms of our problems. Sometimes the Spirit within gives clear evidence of a knowledge and wisdom beyond our own. A Catholic priest friend, for example, was very active in the Charismatic Renewal. He was afraid that the bishop would not accept his place within the movement or the movement itself. I suggested that he take his journal and write. The conversation he had was incredibly supportive and told him exactly what the bishop's reaction would be, a reaction which had never occurred to him to hope for. The next day in his meeting with the bishop, everything occurred just as his inner dialogue had predicted, and he was duly impressed.

Very few people who say that they believe in prayer really believe that it is a two-way street and that God can respond to our needs, our questions, our fears, and our doubts, or fill our hearts with joy. It is helpful to have a record of our experiences to go back to and reflect on. If I simply have this record in my memory and do not write it in my journal, it is too easy to dismiss the entire encounter as wishful thinking. It is much more difficult to dismiss the pencil marks on a piece of paper, particularly when they have spoken the truth about us and the world around us.

We can easily forget such conversations. But as I look back over my journal, I am impressed by the reality and power of these encounters. They have had a greater and more lasting impact on me than all but the most important outer events.[11]

Accepting Unconditional Divine Love: Loving Ourselves as the Christ Loves Us

One main reason for our conflicts with others and our separation from them is that we do not love and value ourselves. Much of our tragic human situation is the result of the failure of human beings to value themselves. When we do not value ourselves as God values us, we poison our relations with others. But the first reaction of most people when I make this suggestion is something like this: "But wouldn't we be egotistical and selfish if we loved ourselves? Isn't this advice just the opposite of Christianity?"

No, strangely enough when we really love ourselves — when we come to terms with ourselves and accept our own weaknesses, foibles, sins and guilts — we do not become selfish and egotistical. Quite the contrary occurs. Once we have come to value ourselves and genuinely like what we are in spite of the ugliness and sinfulness we find within ourselves, then we are free to like others as well, and to treat them as fellow human beings. Once we have come to have a genuine regard for ourselves, then we don't always have to be defensive by drawing attention to the faults of others. We don't have to protect our own egos with a shield of anger toward others. Then we are no longer worried about how others may be talking about us, for we know how we stand with ourselves and God, and what others say isn't going to throw us off balance. We won't be hurt over a slight or injury, because we know the other person probably didn't mean it. And even if he or she did mean it, then it was just a piece of poor judgment on the other's part.

When we basically like the core of our own being, when we accept ourselves and know that God loves us, then if others don't share our opinion, it simply shows that their taste is poor. We have the inside story on ourselves. Once we have been able to like ourselves in spite of what we know, then the uninformed opinions of others no longer bother us. And then the most wonderful thing can happen: We can forget about ourselves and reach out to others and think about them and what concerns them and how they react. Jesus was certainly right when he quoted a famous passage from scripture: "Love your neighbor as yourself," he said, implying very clearly that we cannot love our neighbor until we have loved ourselves. Jesus touched the very heart of the problem in these words. Those who cannot accept themselves as they are seldom are able to care genuinely for their neighbor.

Honesty

As a practical matter, then, how can we come to love ourselves? Our first task — if we are ever to accept ourselves and become free from bitterness and rage toward ourselves and others — is to be honest with ourselves. We cannot possibly love what we do not know. We cannot love ourselves until we are honest with ourselves and see what we actually are. This is painful and difficult, but there is no other way to self-acceptance. When we hate other people, we are projecting our inner anger onto them; this saves us from having to look at the violence within us, which is so difficult to bear. Whenever we violently dislike some quality in another person, we can be almost certain that we are seeing in them something which we can't bear in ourselves.

Until we can bear the pain of looking at what we are, there is little hope of our accepting and valuing what we actually are, and thus little hope of our coming to value any other person in a real way. There are some specific ways that we can be honest with ourselves. We need to take time out to be quiet just with ourselves, without any activity or busyness or T.V. that keep us from being still and waiting for something more. We can also reflect on our reactions to others. We can listen to our dreams. We can talk these things over with someone we trust. Personally I find that if I don't have someone to talk with — someone I trust, who can look at me objectively and see my faults and virtues — I often remain unconscious of them. There is no beginning of any truly loving relation between two people until we are honest with ourselves. Only then can we hope to care for others as they are. We no longer complain about the specks in others' eyes when we have seen clearly the logs in our own eyes.

Admitting Our Worth

The next step is to realize that it is just as morally wrong to dislike, to hate and devalue, to despise and derogate ourselves as it is to have these feelings for other human beings — maybe worse. And — what may come as a shock — this is exactly what Christianity seems to say. Let me put this imaginatively. We are like silly children cooped up in one room of a great house. We do not feel good enough for the mansion, and so we go off into this tiny cell of self-abasement, and there we call to God to come and help us. Love comes and says to us, "Come out of this little room and inherit your vast mansion. This is only a cellar chamber, and the whole place is yours." But we look up and say, "Oh, Lord, but we are not worthy." Then Love is annoyed and says sternly: "How dare you call unworthy the one for whom I died, to whom I come now. You have to abandon this silly attitude or creep back into that cell by yourself and stay there. I know what is worthy, and I came and died for you, and I come when anyone calls me.

Let go of your proud unworthiness. Come with me and inherit the kingdom prepared for you from the foundation of this world. Seeing yourselves as only evil is disillusioned egotism."

If we see no basic value in ourselves, if we persist in hating ourselves, we are politely telling the Holy One that Christ did not know what he was doing in coming to us as a baby in a stable. We know better than God. But this is the mystery of our faith, the great mystery of our Christian experience: that God loves even me and would have died on the cross in Christ Jesus even if I had been the only human on earth. I don't know why this is so, but I do know that this is the way that God sees us. How dare we, then, hate ourselves, whom God values in such an extraordinary way?

Accepting Pardon

Our next endeavor — if we are ever to love ourselves and be free to love others — is to have the courage to accept the forgiveness of others. Yes, I said what I meant: *to accept the forgiveness of others*. It is far easier to forgive than to be forgiven — to forgive than to accept forgiveness. In the Sermon on the Mount, Jesus made this very point: "So when you are offering your gift at the altar, if you remember that your brother or sister has something against you, leave your gift there before the altar and go; first be reconciled to your brother or sister, and then come and offer your gift." He did not say, "If you have something against your brother or sister, go and be reconciled," but rather, "If you remember that your brother or sister has something against you." In other words, if you have done something to another for which you have not tried to receive forgiveness, or for which you have not accepted forgiveness, then Jesus says you should leave your gift before the altar and go and seek forgiveness (cf. Mt 5:23-24).

I once had a very close friend offend me, so much so that I was deeply hurt. But I forgave that friend. Even so, something happened to our friendship. We drifted apart, until one day when we were talking I realized that he couldn't accept my forgiveness; he had felt himself unworthy of my friendship and had withdrawn from me. One has to value oneself, love oneself, in order to accept forgiveness, and in accepting forgiveness one comes to a greater measure of this self-valuing. Did you ever realize that the whole Christian Church is built on those who accepted forgiveness and loved the Lord even more? There was Peter who denied him, John who fled from him, Paul who persecuted and tried to destroy his Church, and yet they all accepted the forgiveness of God and became the founders of Christ's Church.

Our last effort in coming to care for ourselves is to take the chance and relate to other human beings even if they betray us —just as Jesus did. We need to come into a real relationship with others, accepting and being accepted, forgiving and being forgiven. We cannot just sit at home alone and come to an acceptance of ourselves. Real self-acceptance is something that is given in the interaction of human beings. We can't stay apart from others and ever come to love or value ourselves. No one is an island. If we try to be islands, we are less than fully human. Only as we live our lives with other human beings, only as we are accepted and accept others (in spite of betrayal and hurt and being let down), only as we have the courage to be ourselves with others, only then does there grow within us an appreciation, an acceptance, a love for ourselves and other people.

In his letters to his brother Theo, Vincent van Gogh expresses his vision of the meaning of love in words as vivid as the colors on his canvases:

> Do you know what frees one
>   from this captivity? It is
>   every deep serious
>   affection. Being friends,
>   being brothers, love,
>   these open the prison
>   by supreme power,
>   by some magic force.
>   Where sympathy
>   is renewed,

life is restored.
Love a friend, a wife,
something, whatever you like,
but one must love
with a lofty and serious intimate sympathy,
with strength, with intelligence,
and one must always try
to know deeper, better,
and
more.[12]

The Art of Holy Listening

We have already seen that listening is an essential part of kindness and patience. Listening is also modest, gracious, considerate and confidential. Deep listening is only possible where genuine trust can be developed. Human beings vary greatly, and unless we know how to listen to many different people, we have a tendency to assume that other people have the same values as we do and look at the world in the same way we do. I have been listening to people individually and in groups for over fifty years, and I have never met two people who are exactly the same. The stories that people tell about their lives are astonishingly different.[13]

Learning to listen is a key that unlocks the door to loving people. Listening is vital because we can only love those human beings to whom we listen — and, as we have seen, love is the heart of the spiritual journey. And even more significant is the truth that people who do not first learn to listen to other human beings rarely learn to listen to the still, small voice of God. Those who have not learned to listen, seldom learn to love either human beings or God. But what is the nature of the mysterious power of listening? The first step in practicing listening is recognizing its incredible importance in the art of Christian love.

What Is Holy Listening?

Listening is *being silent with another person in an active way*. It is silently bearing with another person. Some people are silent, but they are not open and active. They are either asleep or dead within themselves. The true listener is one who is quiet and yet sensitive toward another person, open and active, receptive and alive. Listening is participating in another life in a most creative and powerful way. It is neither coercive nor pushy. Rather, it is bearing one another's burdens.

The first step in listening is obvious: We must cease talking ourselves. And it is hard for most of us human beings to halt our chatter. No part of our body is more difficult to control than the tongue. It seems at times to have a life of its own, a life quite independent of our rational control.

Too much chatter is usually a form of shyness. We are too insecure to be silent; we use a wall of words to insulate ourselves from others. If we talk enough, we can prevent people from touching us and avoid real communion with others. Continuous talk achieves the same result as social isolation: It obstructs real contact with other human beings and therefore with life itself. Inability to stop talking is a form of unconsciousness or egotism and can lead to serious spiritual and psychological difficulties. Constant chatter is very seldom loving.

Being Silent with Others

The second step in listening, then, is allowing oneself to be with other people and to be silent with them. We are silent not only with our lips but also in our inner response. We listen to the other and are silent inside. We neither agree nor disagree with what is said. We simply listen openly, permitting the other person to be what he or she is, and that freely. Listening is free and open; it does not need to control what is heard, does not need to censor it.

Those who can listen become more secure within themselves.

They know where they stand and what they believe. They become less easily upset or shocked. Some people cannot read
books with which they do not agree. They must fight with the
author and so can get little value from what is written. Such
people find it difficult to listen to someone who has different
ideas or who has done things of which they disapprove. These
are people who are not secure in their own beliefs; they fear that
the ground may be pulled out from under their feet, and so they
dare not listen without emotional and verbal reactions, without
vociferous dissent — as if opinion expressed with emotion were
a protection. We need to develop an inner security in order to
listen deeply. It can be embarrassing to be silent with another,
but it can also be helpful, as I have shown earlier.

The Listener Benefits

There is another strange truth about listening. The people who
learn to listen also strengthen their own convictions and broaden
the base of their faith. By a deep and mysterious chemistry of the
spirit, the listener is established in life and given roots that reach
down into the heart of things. Real listening establishes faith and
confidence. It begins by an act of will and ends by reinforcing the
will that began it.

Those who listen creatively, however, do not remain always
silent. Instead they *reflect with* the other person, to use the term
of Carl Rogers. They amplify and clarify what the speaker says.
They may ask for more detail, but always with the intention of
finding out what is in the other person and of bearing it with him
or her. Genuine listening is never artificial or stilted. It is warm,
interested, concerned, alive. It seeks to know and to care. Listening is love in action.

On another level, real listening is a kind of prayer, for as we
listen, we penetrate through the human ego and hear the Spirit
of God, which dwells in the heart of everyone. Real listening,
then, is a religious experience. Often, when I have listened deeply
to another, I have the same sense of awe as when I am alone in

the church at night. I have entered into a holy place and communed with the heart of being itself. I also marvel at the wonderful variety and mystery of the human beings the Holy One has created and at the amazing way the divine love touches our lives.

Bearing with the Beginnings

We seldom find this deeper level in another's human being until we first are able to listen to the more superficial levels of that person. We must be willing to hear about all the person's petty concerns and interests and desires and hopes. We must listen to descriptions of events that have been meaningful and sad to that person. As we do this, we bear with another human ego in its narrowness and pettiness, in its frustrations and hopes.

If we can learn to do this, then as we listen carefully and watch closely, we will begin to hear that person make a tentative statement of something more. It comes very slowly and gently. We find that the other is trying to let us into a deeper and more sensitive level of his or her being. The novel experience of being listened to has raised the person's hope that perhaps there is another who cares after all — one who can understand. Certainly people can never believe that we care about them until we listen to them.

When the other person is satisfied by these first tentative tests of our acceptance, then the floodgates open and all of the person's inner self pours out — that person's entire being with guilts and faults and sins, with a sense of despair and inadequacy and loneliness, with a self-hatred and self-judgment and inner psychic pain. This is hard for us to bear, for all of us have these dark areas of our souls; to hear of another's darkness stirs up our own pain and loneliness. Attentive listening, therefore, is very hard work; it is difficult to carry the pain and guilt of others. We need times of rest after we listen to many troubled people.

Yet if we do not listen to others' dark side, we never see them in depth. They remain for us like a child's painting, with no shadow or perspective. A friend of mine, who had revealed to me the worst about himself, decided henceforth to carry his burdens by himself. He might just as well have stayed away, since I no longer knew him. Finally he realized what he was doing and wrote me, acknowledging that we can only know others when we know their darkness as well as their light.

When I was teaching at Notre Dame, I let it be known that I had office hours, and I would be glad to discuss any problems the students might have with their courses. I discovered a pattern as graduate and undergraduate students began to make appointments. During the first visit they would most likely bring a book with them. We would talk about the book for a while, and when the students discovered that I would listen to them, I found that the book was only an excuse for coming. Our conversations with them strayed to other subjects. Many of them would make another appointment. This time they carried no book to discuss; they had discovered that I would listen. Soon real concerns would emerge: Their parents talked only about their long hair and made no mention of the fact that they had a 3.7 grade point average. When I passed this test, they would come in to talk about their dating problems. Then floodgates did indeed open. Their deepest and most personal fears and actions poured out. However, it was only during the last few weeks before graduation that many made appointments to reveal their *deepest secret*, their religious experiences.

Listening in Groups

For the last thirty years I have been leading conferences and retreats on deepening the spiritual life. It quickly became clear to me that a Christian conference was not loving and so not truly Christian until people were given an opportunity to talk and listen to each other. We are very seldom given an opportunity to share our life stories with others who also wish to share and listen. In order to create an environment where no individual would be lost in a large group, the conference organizers designed what we called Life Story Groups, which people were invited but not compelled to attend. Each group had a trained listener-leader. A large number of the people attending the conferences were professional church workers, and for many of them this was the first time that they had ever had an opportunity to tell their stories — amazing stories, as amazing as any that I ever heard in private or read in novels. In the evaluations which the retreatants filled out for us, they consistently noted that the small sharing groups were among the most valuable parts of the conference for them. In these groups *they could even share their religious experiences with one another.*

When possible, the groups were formed with an equal number of men and women. Those with close relationships were placed in different groups so they would feel more free to share. At the first group meetings, the following statement was handed out, read, and agreed upon, and to the best of my knowledge, no one ignored the statement's guidelines. These are good rules for any listener or any Christian fellowship or learning group:

The small group is your community for this event. It is neither a therapy group nor a dream interpretation group, but it is an opportunity to be present to one another. The following guidelines are essential:

1. The material shared within the group is confidential. There is no "expiration date" on maintaining this confidentiality.
2. All are invited to share; no one must share if she or he does not choose to do so.
3. It is important in sharing to center on our own feelings and lives. In focusing on your own story, please do not tell another person's story or confess another person's sins.
4. Please observe good listening skills, i.e., avoid interrupting the person sharing; respond only when she or he has finished; receive the sharing non-judgmentally; avoid trying to heal, convert, or "fix" people.
5. The facilitator can step in if the process goes astray.
6. There is a time limitation. Be mindful that others also have time enough to share.

7. Attendance is essential to the group process. It is expected that you will notify your group facilitator if you are unable to attend. Wearing your name tag will be helpful to everyone.

Temple of the Soul

When we listen on this deep level, we begin to hear strange echoes, to see lights, and to catch the strains of a mysterious music of the soul. When we can accept the darkness and ugliness in another, we see beyond it a beauty that we never dreamed existed. We then touch the deepest levels of the incredible human psyche where dwells the spirit of the living Christ, the Holy Spirit, a reality of the greatest power and love and beauty who will guide us into the deepest reaches of the spiritual world. Indeed, as we listen to another, listening with courage to the demonic darkness that is found in all of us, then suddenly the veil lifts and we find that within another human being we have communion with God, the Holy One.

It makes no difference how depraved or how simple a person is; this person contains a central fortress of the soul wherein dwells God. That is why all of us are so valuable, so incalculably valuable that no one may ever be used as a means, but only as an end. There is something divine in every human being, and in listening fully we come into communion with the Holy.

As we learn to listen to people and find this element in them, we come to love them with divine charity, because they are God-bearers. We are awed, utterly awed, by the mystery and depth of the human soul that carries within it a spirit such as this. Indeed, I doubt if anyone ever really penetrates into the deepest recesses of another soul without experiencing this awe. Something instinctive in us keeps this level closed to any except for those who develop such reverence, those who can listen in holy awe. Obviously, when we have this kind of reverence for others, we do not repeat what they have told us. What we have heard becomes our holy secret, except when we have been given permission to share what we have been told.

Those who discover such a spirit dwelling in the human psyche find that they are also able to relate to that spirit directly. But seldom do we find this ability, seldom do we hear the still small voice of God, until we first learn to open ourselves to other human beings. Many years ago Rudolf Steiner put it well: "Only to those, who by selfless listening train themselves to be really receptive within, in stillness, unmoved by personal opinion or feeling, only to such can the higher beings speak. . . . As long as one hurls any personal opinion or feeling against the speaker to whom one must listen, the beings of the spiritual world remain silent." In addition, one who has found such a spirit within all of us human beings knows that human beings are of supreme value, that no person can be treated as a thing or an it.

The value of such listening is beyond words. All genuine human relationships are based upon it. Indeed, human communication and fellowship are utterly impossible without it. How can we love and deal creatively with a person we do not know? How can we know someone to whom we have not listened? The ability to listen, therefore, is a prerequisite to love. All creative human relationship begins with listening and continues with actions of thoughtfulness and love.

Unless we listen to human beings, we do not know what they are. So we treat them as what we think they are, rather than as what they really are. In such cases, we project either positive or negative elements of ourselves upon other human beings and try to force them into the patterns that we think they ought to conform to. This may be a kind of communication with ourselves, but it is certainly no communication with the other person and no basis for real relationship.

To Whom Do We Listen?

We human beings all have a gift to share. We need to listen to those who most need to be heard by us. Our first priority will be listening to our children, to our husbands or wives, to our more extended families and to our intimate friends. We can cause real

damage to those who belong within the inner circle of relationships if we neglect or avoid listening to them. Our neighbors,
employees, employers, social contacts, the clerk in the store,
people we meet at church, or the person who delivers the paper
can be others to whom we can give our gift of listening. We never
know when a piece of hardened mud will contain jewels within.
Then there is the stranger whom providence puts in our pathway,
and even the enemy: We have to reach out even to these people
if we are to be instruments of love and listening. Some people are
called to reach out to the homeless, the poor, those in prison, the
hungry and thirsty, the dying and the defeated. If we cannot do
this kind of listening and loving, we can at least support those
who are called to this service to Christ.

Let us look at the special ways we can listen to and love those
close to us, those neighbors who are farther from us, and those
who are painful to deal with. Let us also realize that we cannot
carry all those who could use our love and listening; we need to
decide carefully which ones we are called to minister to without
neglecting our first priorities in love.

Loving Special Neighbors

Divine love treats each individual as a unique and special person. If we are following the way of Jesus' love, we need to give each individual appropriate, considerate understanding and kindness. We have already noted that people are born and grow from infancy through childhood and adolescence to adulthood, to a wider spiritual understanding, to a golden age and then on to a time of preparation for eternal life. Every person at every stage requires different expressions of love. We all grow up with different backgrounds and hurts and hopes and fears. We need, therefore, to know about others before we pour out our love upon them. We need to listen to them and respond to their special needs. A bubbly, happy person can cause pain and discouragement to one who is lost in darkness. Love never argues with a person who is struggling; it never tells anxious people, "Just snap out of it." Love hears and responds to the pain of others. The author of "O Little Town of Bethlehem," Phillip Brooks, said: "Be kind, for everyone is carrying a heavy burden." Love seeks to know and bear those burdens; it also seeks to accompany satisfied people to greater joy, love, service and peace.

Human beings find themselves in a wide range of situations. The way we share love with our husband or wife will be different from the way we share love with our children in each of their different stages of development. In any case, we have an unavoidable responsibility to love our families; if we do not give love to them, they can be deeply damaged for life.

The love we share with family, friends and acquaintances will differ from the expression of love given to strangers. In addition, Jesus told his disciples many times that they would not understand the deepest form of love until they learned to love their enemies. In order to deal with enemies, however, we have to look at the anger that often separates us from them. We also need to find methods of expressing love to the starving, hurting children and adults all over the world — neighbors as near to us as the television screen in the living room. And we need to see how we can protect our fragile blue planet, earth. God created this incomparable gift so that we might have a home that could give us birth and nurture our every need. Unless we protect it, we show our children's children little love.

These are enormous problems. Let us look at them one by one. The reader may wish to look at only one at a time, as the totality of these problems can be overwhelming.

Loving Our Families

As we open ourselves to divine unconditional love, we can begin to understand what kind of love needs to pour through us to those in the inner circle of our relationships, our family and our closest friends. This would seem perfectly obvious, but as anyone finds who listens as a marriage counselor, love is seldom greater in so-called Christian families than among today's pagans. Yet families that are short on love are spawning grounds for nearly every human problem. In the words of one writer on the subject, "There are no panderers, procurers and pimps so cunning and irresistible as those parents who themselves have not experienced love."[1]

Jesus simply assumes that we will love our families, our children, wives, husbands, our brothers and parents — even as good heathens do. Let us look again at what he said about this in the Sermon on the Mount: "If you love only those who love you, what reward can you expect? Surely the tax-gatherers do as much as that. And if you greet only your brothers, what is there extraordinary about that? Even the heathen do as much" (Mt 5:46). It never occurred to Jesus that he should have to tell us to love those who love us. And yet, looking at Christian families today, one does not even see continuous love within them. So Christians who do not love their own families are not even as morally advanced as the heathens and tax-collectors, the harlots and sinners of Jesus' time. Isn't it more than a little shocking to find the general run of Christian families little more loving than anyone else? How has this come about? I have a theory.

The ancient pagans were taught to love their friends and family with a burning love and to hate their enemies with a violent hatred. They worked at both. When they had heathen friends, they were friends forever, and these friends could count on their loyalty until hell froze over. But after Christianity became the accepted religious idea of the Western world, people were taught not to hate, and so they pretended that they did not hate anyone. As a result, the hatred in them dropped down into the depth within them; it was forgotten and ignored in the unconscious. There it worked autonomously and silently. The hatred began to come out where it was least expected, even unnoticed, upon loved ones. In fact, families and loved ones have often had the treatment once reserved for enemies.

Besides this, the followers of Christ were saddled with another unique idea — the idea of the equality and value of women, and also of the value of children just as children, not as adults-to-be. For this reason, Christian marriage and family life require a mutuality and respect which is hard for us human beings. We must be quite conscious, quite aware to get along in a mutual relationship. This differs radically from the kind of family in which one member or another is the titular head of the house — a family structure which avoids the need for and stress on mutual relationships.

No other religious leader of humankind has placed as much value on women and children as Jesus of Nazareth did. He valued them as much as men. Jesus saw love and equality to be the basis of family life.

Dr. Carl Jung once made a brief but pointed comment on this whole family issue. A friend was telling him about a certain man and what a saint he was; Jung, with a twinkle in his eye, retorted, "Oh? But I would want to know his wife and children before I decided on his sainthood." It turns out that the man's wife was a basket case. Thus, we Christians, it seems, need to consider how to love our families, as well as loving ourselves as Christ loves us. My first suggestion, then, for those of us who wish to develop familial love is that we recognize clearly that our first priority in love needs to be our spouses and children and even our parents.

Showing Affection

My second suggestion is simply *to show one's natural and ordinary feelings of affection and love when one feels them and not be afraid of these feelings.* Many people I know are able to express negative or hostile feelings, but either cannot or do not show any of the positive and loving movements of the heart. In the fourth century Ambrose, in a book on the duties of the clergy, gave his ministers some of the finest advice on how one can help Christian love to grow. Ambrose wrote:

> It gives a very great impetus to mutual love if one shows love in return to those who love us and proves that one does not love them less than oneself, especially if one shows it by the proof that a faithful friendship gives. What is so likely to win favor as gratitude? What more natural than to love one who loves us? What so implanted and so impressed upon a person's feelings as the wish to let others, by whom we want to be loved, know that we love them? Well does the wise man say: "Lose thy money for thy brother and thy friend," and again, "I will not be ashamed to defend a friend, neither will I hide myself from him."

And in discussing the popularity of King David, Ambrose remarked: "Who would not have loved him, when they saw how dear he was to his friends? For as he truly loved his friends, so he thought that he was loved as much in return by his own friends. Because of his love to his friends, people put David above their own families and children."[2]

Thoughtfulness

A third way of showing that we love our family is by simple kindness and thoughtfulness, by doing little acts of kindness and sentiment. We all enjoy being remembered by a little gift or some flowers. Children greatly enjoy a toy from father or mother returning from a trip. How seldom we do even this much! In marriage counseling, I hear many women complain that they are simply taken for granted; the husband never remembers special days, never does extra kindnesses. And husbands have a similar complaint: "I am nothing but a bank account." Simply stopping to think about each other and doing some small act of remembrance and caring does wonders. *All of us* are insecure, and we all need some little display of affection and interest in us to give us value and worth. We are hardly human if we need no acts of caring from others. One trouble is that we get so caught up, each in our worthlessness, that we minister to no one, and so no one ministers to us. We receive love most often when we give love.

Time Together

Love cannot be expressed to those we love, however, without the expenditure of time. If we really care — or want to care — about someone, then we will spend time with that person alone. Time with a wife or friend in the company of others does not have the same value as time alone with the person we wish to relate to. *Too often we take those we love for granted and simply deny them the time that is needed for relationship.* Relationship can never be given in a pill or a gift. One help that I have found is to have dinner out alone with my wife or child or friend. One hour alone like this is worth twenty with that person in a group. Susanna Wesley, the mother of John and Charles Wesley, had twenty children, and she managed to spend an hour a week alone with each of them. Eleven of the children became religious, political and literary figures in eighteenth-century England. If we want to show love to our families, we will have some time alone with each member. Group experience is important, but individual time with each parent and child is even more important; one does not take the place of the other.

Then, as we take this time, we will listen to each other. Love always desires to find out about the other person; love is interested in the events of the day, the thoughts, desires, fears, even the angers of the other. If love is genuine, it cares, and caring always involves listening. As Louis Evely has put it so beautifully in *That Man Is You*:

> Love must express and communicate itself. . . .
> That's its nature. . . .
> When two people begin to love one another,
> they start telling everything that's happened to them,
> every detail of their daily life:
> they "reveal" themselves to each other,
> unbosom themselves and exchange confidences. . . .
> God hasn't ceased being revelation . . .
> any more than he's ceased being love.
> He enjoys expressing himself.
> Since he's love, he must give himself,
> share his secrets . . . communicate
> with us . . . and reveal himself to
> anyone who wants to listen.[3]

Without listening there is no communication, and without communication there is no love. Each of us needs to be listened to, to be found by another who loves us as we are. Some of the brightest and wisest married people have not *made* time for each other. So my fourth suggestion is that each parent *make* at least an hour a week alone with each family member.

The Power of Touch

We live in a society that has become neurotic about touch and, of course, touch that is forced upon another or is inappropriate is not acceptable behavior. Suggestive language is also demeaning and is not proper. However, we have also noted that many infants who are not cuddled and held wither away and die. (Even orphan chimpanzees who are not brought up with tangible relationships with other chimps do not know how to respond to their fellow chimps. They have to be taught just like human children. Loving them teaches them to love.[4]) When the show of affection ceases within a family, both children and adults know that something is wrong; love is not drawing them together. This is particularly true among fathers and sons. Many of the students at Notre Dame asked me why their fathers suddenly stopped giving them hugs or laying a hand on their shoulders when they reached a certain age.

One brilliant and successful man confided in me that the only time his father touched him as a child was when he was spanked. Those who have never received affectionate touch find it difficult to give it. We are not talking about intimate, sexual touch; that is an entirely different subject.[5]

Jesus often used touch in his healing ministry. The apostles and their followers used the laying-on-of-hands and anointing with oil to carry out his ministry. This ministry continued up until the time of the Reformation in the West and still continues in the Eastern Orthodox Church. After Vatican II, anointing for healing and the laying-on-of-hands have become much more widespread in the Catholic Church and also more frequent in some Protestant denominations. The healing ministry is sacramental touch. Leòn Joseph Cardinal Suenens has been active in the ministry of spiritual gifts and particularly in the healing ministry.[6]

A psychiatrist friend told me a remarkable example of the power of touch. For a long time he had seen a woman patient whose condition had not improved very much. Then one day she was so nearly well that, after a visit or two, she no longer needed to see him. Some time later they happened to meet at a social gathering. My friend studied her face quietly for a moment, and then asked, "Would you tell me? What was it that made you well? Was it anything that I did?" And with a quick smile, she told him, "Oh, I thought you knew. When my son was critically ill in the contagious ward in the hospital, and I was waiting in the corridor for news, you came by and stopped to ask about him. You put your hand on my shoulder, and I knew that you cared. It was then that I started to get better. Before that incident I had not thought anyone could care for me."

Touch can convey to others that we really care. But our caring also needs to be conveyed in words. Each day we need to express to those in our family how much they mean to us, how much we care. Usually there is laughter at a conference when I tell the story of the Iowa farmer whose wife was constantly complaining about how seldom he said that he loved her. One Sunday after dinner he heard the familiar complaint. He got up and said: "My dear, when I married you, I told you that I loved you. If it changes, I will let you know." Can you imagine a couple living together who really love each other and never speak of it or touch one another? Verbal communication and touch are two of the simplest and yet most important ways of expressing our feelings of love and concern. They feed the soul. So my fifth suggestion for the development of familial love is that we make an effort by word and touch to increase family bonds of affection and love. We need to find several occasions every day to express our love to one another. Love nourishes love.

Unconditional Support

If we really love those within the family circle, we will also stand up for them when they are subjected to condemnation from the world or from themselves. Our acceptance and praise are much more likely to give strength, direction and solid morality than judgment or criticism, ridicule or physical punishment. So often our judgment of children is the projection upon them of our own fears and insecurities. As Van der Post has put it, "One cannot just pick out what one likes in people and reject the rest. That's using people, not loving them."[7]

This is particularly true of children as they come to the period when they must meet new experiences on their own terms. It is certainly not easy for us as parents when sons and daughters begin to have their own ideas and to rebel against us. But only with our acceptance and love can they be helped to express the hostility and frustration within them so that it does not become unconscious and destructive.

Years ago I knew two social workers who adopted two children from an orphanage and tried to raise them in a rational, objective way. Within a year the children had to be sent back because they were incorrigible. Then the couple took two others, and this time they made their home the children's fortress; with firmness and love, they supported the children in all they did. Every one of us needs a place where we are accepted and considered valuable whether we are right or wrong. Real friends or parents are those who are behind us whether we are right or wrong, just because they are our friends or parents. If we love those within our family, we will be with them no matter what they are or do. We will also express appreciation and admiration for them. And we will find something to praise — for the world gives praise far too seldom.

Unconditional support, then, is a sixth way to express love within the family. This kind of concern, loyally and persistently *expressed*, is necessary if we are ever to have families in which love can grow and from which our love and concern can spread out into the world. Christianity is an extension of this pagan virtue of family love, but it cannot grow until we do at least as well as the pagans. When this love is based upon such a dogged, determined, loyal expression of unconditional support within Christian families, then we can sincerely reach out with love beyond our families to the pagan world in which we live.

Loving the Acquaintance

Most of the people with whom we come in contact in our lives are neither strangers nor family nor close friends; they are, rather, people whom we know casually. How do we express *agape* love to them? What is appropriate? We do not want to express indifference on the one hand, but we do not wish to give the idea that they are close friends either. As a clergy person I am able to call on any member of the parish, and I also feel free to be with people who were not members of the parish at all. Most people, however, shudder when representatives of certain religious sects come to their door; the idea of lay ministry — the priesthood of all true believers — has been lost in most of our Churches. In the early Church, members of the persecuted fellowship of Christians had to be careful, but they were nonetheless willing to share the message of Jesus and his resurrection with those who were interested — even if it meant torture and death.

At seminary we were trained in what our professors thought we should know. This was largely Bible study, theology and the history of the Church. But there was little training in how to share our knowledge or in pastoral care, and even less in organizing lay people to spread the good news of the Holy One's incredible love for us humans. Through the work of Gordon Cosby, head of the Church of the Savior, I have come to see that one of the main tasks of the clergy is to train lay people to minister. The Church of the Savior, with no more than 150 members, has developed incredible ministries in the slums of Washington. Gordon Cosby, like John Wesley, realized that Christians need to meet in small groups in which they pray together, work out their problems together, and are united in some kind of ministry. The same provision for small groups was provided by Benedict in the profound *Rule of St. Benedict.* The same basic methods have had phenomenal success in South Korea, where belonging to the Church means participation in small group fellowship, prayer and ministry. Carlo Carretto wrote: "Jesus came to bring fire not the catechism to the earth." This "fire" is the fire of love.

I was first exposed to the principle of group caring, love for the acquaintance, not by a theologian but by a businessman trying to restore a failing manufacturing company. Jack Smith (his real name) was the president of a medium-sized manufacturing plant. The business had been started by his father and had grown. Finally the tension of running the business became too much for the father, and so he turned the business over to his son.

Things continued to go well after World War II, but then for several reasons the market began to shrink, and the quality of the product began to deteriorate.

One day in the midst of these difficulties Jack Smith was in the factory trying to settle a disagreement between two employees, who were arguing about whether it was too hot or too cold — with no thermometer in sight. This was the final straw. Smith left the factory, went into his office, closed the door, sat down at his desk, closed his eyes and said to himself, "I can't run this business. I don't know what to do. I guess I can either get drunk or I can pray." He thought a little while longer and then reflected quietly: "Probably nothing will change if I pray. But if I get drunk, nothing will change either, and I'll have a hangover. And if I pray and nothing comes of it, I can always get drunk later on." With this deep conviction he put his head down on his hands and said, "Okay, Lord, I can't run this business any longer. What should I do?"

He was quiet a few moments and suddenly these words shot through his head in rapid fire: "Create the conditions whereby individuals can develop to the maximum of their capacities within the opportunities at hand." He was thunderstruck and responded out loud: "What was that, Lord?" This time the same sentence spoke itself in slowly measured words in his mind. He wrote it down. I have never come across a better description than this of the way to love employees, employers, students, teachers, members of the Holy Name Society or people in the PTA. This statement also gives the clue to caring (loving) relations with people attending conferences, members of the bridge club, our golfing companions or clerks in a store. Our task is to provide an atmosphere, as much as it is within our hands to do so, in which other people can grow, to the maximum of their spiritual-loving potential.

Jack Smith was impressed by this experience. He did not realize at the time that the insight which had come to him was also the most recent management theory developed by professional managers in business. He decided, however, that if God could still speak, he should take the New Testament seriously. He started almost immediately to examine it carefully, and he read it through seven times. After doing so, he began to realize that this answer to his prayer made sense. The company was little more than the people who worked there, and if each of them was working, thinking, creating, caring for others at top potential, then the company would grow and prosper. His task as primary influence in this organization was to create an atmosphere in which human beings could grow and develop. He also realized that this principle applied not only to the employees whom he liked, or who liked him, but to all of those who worked at the company.

Eleven Suggestions for Love in Action

But how was he to create that positive climate among his employees? For many months he allowed his new insight to ferment in the depth of him. Gradually he came to the conclusion that he must apply as many of Christ's teachings to the practical, everyday concerns of his business as possible. This would not only be good business; it would also be Christianity in action, love actualized within the workplace. One day as he was meditating on how to accomplish this goal, eleven guidelines emerged from the depth of him just as the original insight about management had come to him. Here is his list:

1. Serve those whom you expect to serve you.
2. Consider no person inferior, but recognize limitations.
3. Lead men and women by action and example.
4. Be humble in speaking about your accomplishments.
5. Teach and be taught.
6. Attack unfairness from any quarter.
7. Believe that your employees must prosper if you are to prosper.
8. Seek the truth no matter who may get hurt.
9. Pray for God's guidance when you must make a decision affecting the life and future of any person.

10. Make your own decision based on your own best judgment only after careful consideration has been given to *all* the facts.
11. Forgive honest mistakes where the person making the mistake is honestly self-critical. If people are not self-critical, they must learn to be or they can never successfully supervise others or develop to their best abilities.

This is quite a set of suggestions. In effect they provide a base for treating human beings as persons rather than as objects, as *thou* rather than *it*. These ideas were successfully tested by this company as a basis for both personal and industrial growth. Let's look at some of the implications of these rules.

First, by seeing ourselves as serving, we will develop along with others in the group. We also need to look honestly at individuals and their personal abilities (including our own); we must not just judge people according to the positions they fill or by comparing their results with what *we* do. It is our job to examine our own actions, our own example, and to try to understand the actions of others in the context of the total situation in which we work. We can neither toot our own horn nor force others into impossible roles beyond their limitations. We need to teach by our own example, and listen, watch and learn from each individual. To do this, every individual must be treated as a person who can grow and develop in his or her own right. Most of us do not start to develop freely until we are treated in this way by people who want to share their experience and knowledge with us.

Fairness, Truth and Forgiveness

On the other hand, it hurts the individual, as well as souring group relations, to tolerate unfairness from any source. And if we are truly fair, we will want others to prosper as we are trying to. Equally, to put our own or anyone else's judgment about persons or things above the truth causes unfairness, and individuals are hurt far more when this attitude persists than when facts are sought and truth is faced squarely. Who do we think we are to make our own truth? When we do this, we make ourselves more than God and reality. Indeed, much injury and pain and misunderstanding would be avoided if we insisted on the two standards of *fairness* and *truth*. And the only place to start is with our own determination to seek the facts and to pray to God from the depth of our being whenever we must come to a decision affecting every human being. We also need a spiritual companion or friend with whom we can talk, one who shares Jesus' views of love and will be honest with us. If we seek the truth and listen to what comes in the silent recesses of the soul and to feedback from an objective friend with the same ideals, we will usually come to understand what is the best course of action for all concerned.

Finally, when we give others the freedom to make mistakes, we give them the freedom to grow. It is often only by mistakes — which all of us make — that we grow and develop. We need to offer forgiveness to those who make mistakes; we also need to help them, by forgiving them and by recognizing their positive abilities, to understand and evaluate their own actions. By developing a self-critical understanding of themselves, people begin to grow to the fullness of their abilities. Without forgiveness, men and women stop growing because they are afraid to make mistakes. Without careful evaluation of themselves, they do not profit from their mistakes.

These principles actually did create an atmosphere in Jack Smith's business that helped individuals grow and develop as the company grew and prospered. But this is not just a business success story. The important moral to this story is that seriously opening ourselves to the voice of God and trying to put caring principles to work can change the spiritual climate and moral atmosphere of any group of which we are a part. This is particularly true of any group in which we are the primary influence.

This is a story of Christianity in action, of Christ moving in our world, told in words that we can understand. It is a Christianity founded on treating every person as having the same value and worth as ourselves. This is what Christ came to teach, for when we do treat people this way, then God is present, breaking into the human heart and becoming known in actual reality. These guidelines apply not only in this one business situation. They apply everywhere — to small businesses, committees, neighborhoods, clubs, casual friendships.

Most neighborhoods would be delightful places to live in if these simple, basic suggestions were followed. Most churches would be truly redeeming fellowships if clergy and congregation agreed to put these rules into action. During the last five years that I was pastor of a large congregation, we tried to use these suggestions in the parish. They worked. In addition, I have found that using these principles as a base for the graduate classroom created an open atmosphere where most students were eager to learn and grow.

Of course, these suggestions need to be varied and applied to the specific situations in which we find ourselves. However, I know of no better way to try to love the acquaintance, the person with whom I am casually and not intimately related, than to create the conditions whereby individuals may develop to the maximum of their potential within the opportunities at hand. I know of no better guidelines for implementing this goal than those which my friend, Jack Smith, shared with me nearly forty years ago. This story also reminds us that praying when we have an intense need is dangerous: We may be answered. Then the responsibility is on our shoulders. The Holy One still wants to help us with our real needs, just as, according to the Acts of the Apostles, divine love spoke and directed a persecuted church and helped it take over the empire that tried to destroy it.

Loving and Liking Our Enemies

Jesus believed that real ascent on the spiritual way does not begin until we start to love our enemies, those who mistreat us, those who spitefully use us. We must love our enemies: There is no question that Jesus said it and taught it and lived it. *We are not to love the enemy instead of the friend and family and acquaintance, but in addition to them.* Other loving is a preparation for this supreme effort. And let no one think that it is not difficult to sincerely love the enemy.

It almost seems unnatural to say that we can love those who persecute us. How can we love those whom we do not like? Is it not hypocrisy, pure and unadulterated, to profess that we love those whom we do not even enjoy being near? No, this is not hypocrisy; it is the way of tension and growth. Starr Daily certainly knew what it was to have lots of enemies after years in and out of prison. He later became an eloquent witness to Christ's love and used to tell me that it was not his friends who made him grow, but his enemies. He had to grow to encompass them.

One conventional way of avoiding the strong medicine of the gospel of love is to maintain that I can love people that I don't like. I don't have to like everyone, some say, but I must love them. Let me say very clearly and simply that loving without liking is not loving at all. Please deliver me from the love of people who do not like me. Genuine love is a quality of caring which finds something appealing in the other person. Not liking — disliking — is a form of judging, and is different from the *agape* Paul describes. We are beginning to follow the way of love, the way of Christ, when our loving and our liking start to converge. This does not imply that we approve of everything that other people are doing, for they may be causing harm and hurt. But we can still care for them and love them.

But how can I begin to love and like my enemy? What can I do to enable me to start toward this seemingly impossible goal? Years of struggling with my own dislikes and fears and angers and hates have produced six suggestions which usually help when I put my energy into working at them.

Facing Our Anger and Hurts

The first absolutely necessary step in starting to love the enemy is to recognize that at present most of us do not register very high on the loving-the-enemy scale. Not only are there people we don't like very well, people we avoid, people we strike back at; sometimes we don't even show an unrelenting effort to love those who are close to us. Often the enemy will pop up right in our own family. There is a lovely quip that one reason children and grandparents get along so well is that they have a common enemy! It is rather shocking to observe how little love we have in our hearts and our lives, how little of our action and behavior is determined by our desire to "like-love" those around us.

One of the most virulent forms of rejection is avoiding people. Studiously avoiding others or ignoring them is usually more hostile and violent than blowing up at them or striking them with our hand. We human beings are social creatures; many of us wither and die when we are out of contact with other humans. We have already observed that, in many cultures, banishment from the country or the social group was considered nearly on a par with a death sentence.

Many years ago my son and some of his friends decided that they would play a trick on one of the members of their little group at school. They carefully, assiduously avoided speaking to this young man from the time they arrived in the morning, and as the day went on, the young man became more and more disturbed. When he left at three o'clock before school was out, he was physically ill. My son and his friends were very much ashamed of themselves and they apologized later, but they learned how important they were to one another. There is probably no way we can hurt others more than by subtly turning our backs on them.

There can be no growth in Christian love until we reflect how little caring there is in most of us much of the time. When we realize this, then we need to decide to try to do better. This is the only way that the finer flowers of love can ever begin to bloom in our lives. We can make a beginning by recognizing that our acts of love are rather puny and then by having the determination to be more heroic in the way of love.

There is one group of people who are especially hard for me to love. These are the people who come up to me at a conference when I am talking about love and smile with saccharine sweetness, saying, "But I don't know what you are talking about. I love everyone and everyone loves me." Except for those cases of first-class saints (and I have met but few in my travels up and down the highways of the world), such people are examples of pure unconsciousness. They are simply unaware of their own inner murderers and inner idiots.

Sometimes our very attempt to love and advance on the spiritual way will actually gain enmity from others. A friend reminded me that Jesus was hung on a cross, most of the prophets were persecuted, Socrates was fed hemlock, and most of the saints came close to condemnation before they were accepted as true saints. There is a touching and realistic scene in one of Charles Williams' poems. When Parsifal meets Lancelot, his somewhat erring father, he asks Lancelot's forgiveness for having lived such an exemplary life, for Parsifal knows that his guiltless life must have added to his father's guilt and pain.

Love may involve suffering as it opens us up to the deep, great heart of the world who carries all our human pain and suffering. Love is redeemed as it leads to the utter joy that is prepared for us in that eternal fellowship with Love that lies on the other side of death.

It is important to remember that enemies are those who do not like us, as well as those whom we do not like. Jesus told us to leave our gift at the altar if we remembered that someone had something against us. We should go and be reconciled and then present our gift.

Often within the Christian family as well as in Christian groups — in guilds and sodalities, in parish councils and vestries, in coffee hours and church suppers — there is an unashamed lack of Christian love. This tragic lack turns many people away from Christianity. Indeed, people sometimes even pride themselves on the fact that they have deep and well-rooted animosities within them. It is one thing for us to have them (all of us do); it is quite another to be proud of them. The first step, then, in our attempt at loving the enemy is to realize that we have enemies. This helps us see where we are in our journey toward Christian wholeness and where we really want to be.

Stopping Our Actions of Anger and Vengeance

The second step toward loving the enemy is equally simple. Without it there can be no increase in our spiritual temperature. That step consists of ceasing to do anything unkind to the enemy. This is so obvious that it should not even be necessary to suggest it. As long as we express our anger or hostility in punitive action, in reprisal or in any form of attack, financial, physical or psychological, there is no hope that our "love-liking" toward that person will increase. These actions wear deeper the rut of our anger so that the wheels of our lives are less able to get out of the groove of hostility. Acts of retribution feed the fire of hatred.

And yet anger is a perfectly natural reaction to the injury and wrong that we so often suffer. Someone kicks me in the shins, and I immediately mobilize my entire being so I can kick that person back, and a little harder to boot. If a neighbor sweeps leaves into my yard, my natural tendency is to go and sweep them right back, and a few more along with them. If my wife complains about something I have done, I look for some worse failing in her and complain back. If people hurt our feelings, we either try to return the hurt or else we turn our backs and quite pointedly give them the cold shoulder.

Jesus told us that we should turn the other cheek and go the second mile with one who forced us to go one mile. He was trying to dramatize the fact that if we are to grow in love, we simply have to cease our destructive actions before we can focus in the right direction. When we begin to consider the possibility of living by these statements from Jesus, at least we will stop our actions of retribution. And then we even discover that Jesus was also showing us a nonviolent way of standing up for ourselves, as Walter Wink points out.[8]

Although most of us are quite civilized in public, many do attack each other at home with bric-a-brac, fists, guns or knives. Of course, the law strongly discourages this behavior in most countries. It is shocking, however, that this kind of violence still takes place within the confines of supposed domestic tranquility.

What we wouldn't think of doing at the club, we do at home. Police find that intervening in domestic quarrels is their most dangerous duty other than tracking down violent criminals. In the public arena, furthermore, we can also be very cruel — usually not in an outwardly violent but rather in a legal, subtle and very refined way. But such aggression is as destructive as a physical attack. So our second step in developing in love for the enemy is to realize that we are indulging in violent or aggressive actions of one kind or another and to *bring these actions to a halt*.

Anger and Hostility Revisited

Even as we realize that we need to bring our unloving actions to a halt, we also need to recognize that anger is a necessary part of being human and can be a source of energy. Anger has dozens of different names. When we are hurt or threatened, we usually have the impulse toward either flight or fight. Anger is the mobilization of our entire being to attack what is threatening us. We often pay a deadly price when we try to forget, repress or ignore our anger.

Emotions are those human responses in which physical and bodily reactions go along with a set of feelings. When we are angry, our bodies prepare for action; bronchial tubes open up to let in more oxygen, blood sugar is released to provide fuel for the oxygen to burn, heartbeat and blood pressure increase to race this energy through the body, and blood-clotting time goes down to prepare for a possible injury. When my friend Tommy Tyson, the well-known evangelist, listened to a recital of the physical effects of anger, he reacted spontaneously with these words: "I can't afford to sit on my anger and let it seethe. It will destroy me. Doing that is immoral."

When bottled up, unfaced anger, resentment and hostility can cause social chaos. The blood feud which is still endemic in many societies or in American street gangs is a perfect example of this. Any little slight (real or imagined) can trigger a monumental reaction. Continued hatred can cause psychological tension, leading to bitterness, isolation and disaster. Repressed hostility can erode our physical bodies as a heavy rain erodes a bare hillside. John Sanford has often said: "It is so stupid to hate people. It ties us to the people we like the least."

What can I do to get this inner energy released in a creative and positive manner? First of all I need to see that anger, except in certain cases of physical danger, seldom produces positive results. As long as I hang onto my anger consciously, I am not following Christ, and I am putting myself in a dangerous position religiously, socially, psychologically and physically.

There are things I can do to get my anger under control. I can write down my anger, concretize it, put it out before me and see what it looks like in black and white as if it were someone else's bitterness. I can talk it over with a friend. I can look for an outer cause of the anger and change what is upsetting me. Sometimes I find that there is little or nothing I can do about a situation which causes anger and resentment down to the marrow of my soul. Then, like Job, I can cry out to God from the depth of my agony. At such times I usually feel the presence of God very keenly, and I know that I have come into contact with one who is able to bear the burden of my anger and distress. As the crucified one, Christ knew this agony himself. When I have protested specifically to God in my journal about the abyss which so often reaches up to suck me down into it, I have found that the risen Christ appears and that the pain and anger have usually subsided by the next day; the abyss has less power to touch me, and sometimes it even disappears.

There is no sin in being angry. The sin is to pretend the anger is not there or to let it out whenever we feel it or to nurse anger in our relationships, feeding the anger with more and more grievances without facing the actual situation honestly and squarely. *Nursed anger becomes hate*: Hatred is evil and destructive and leads to tragedy. In all great tragic drama, hatred has won the day. Then love is defeated in us, because hate is the zero of love. Paul wrote to the Ephesians, "Even if you are angry, you must not sin; never let the sun set on your anger or else you will give the devil a foothold" (4:26). If we are to defeat the anger of the murderer within, we will need to renounce the murderer's way and bring our best effort to bear on changing our pattern of action, replacing the natural angry reaction with a more positive one. And it turns out that *the person I view as an enemy often reveals to me my own inner murderer better than most other people I know.*

Again we need to be reminded that one of the reasons that the Christian Church conquered the ancient world was that it actually practiced this kind of loving attitude toward the enemy. The seed of the Church truly was the blood of the martyrs. The martyrs went to the arena without cursing and breathing vengeance upon the spectators, and the spectators at the arena were stupefied. The Christians thrown to the beasts actually handled their torments as Jesus did on the cross. Saint Perpetua was martyred by wild beasts in North Africa in the second century; when she was asked why she did not curse the informers, the judges, those who were about to put her into the arena and those gathered to watch, she replied, "They already suffer from the attack of the evil one. I do not want to add to their burden with my curses."

Bridling the Tongue

The next suggestion for loving the enemy is an extension of the last one. It concerns a problem so common and so often considered harmless that it requires special attention: *gossip.* Whenever I gossip negatively about others, I am treating them as the enemy. One of the Ten Commandments tells us that we should not bear false witness against our neighbor. This could well be translated: We shall not gossip.

Not only does my unkind action wear deeper the rut of my ugliness, but *my unkind talking about other people does exactly the same thing*. I personally find this step very difficult. The tongue at times seems to have a life all of its own. And yet I know how much I dislike it when I find that others have been discussing me in a critical or gossipy way. When there is a group moral dissection of someone going on and I have a juicy morsel which I could add, I cannot add it without damaging myself. That kind of gossip pushes me away from my goal of love.

I know of only two valid reasons for saying an unkind or critical remark about another person. In the first case my inner feelings of critical anger are hurting me so much that I need to discharge them. However, such things should be expressed to a priest or a spiritual friend and not vented in the heat of the moment upon the enemy or anyone else, especially a child (violent and angry words can be as destructive for children and those close to us as physical torture). The other reason is that we truly believe that the actions of these people may be hurting other persons or themselves, and that they need help. In Matthew 17 we are given detailed instructions on how to handle the latter situation. First of all we are to go to such people directly and see if we can come to an understanding with them. If this does not work, then we are to take two or three with us and try the same method. This failing, we are to go to the Church in order to clear up the circumstances which are causing the problem. And last of all, if those people will not listen to us, we are to treat them as tax gatherers and sinners. We should remember at this point, however, how Jesus treated even tax-gatherers and sinners: He treated them with love and charity and went out to them. They even became his disciples.

Jesus gives us excellent advice in Matthew 17, as I know from experience. Early in my ministry I wrote a note to a woman from the parish who was studying theology in a seminary; it was mistaken for a telegram. A religious leader added two and two, got twenty-two, and concluded that something was going on between me and this woman at the seminary. Instead of coming directly to me, he went to my bishop, who went to the dean, who talked to my wife, who had helped write the note and knew all about it. Had the dean and the bishop not had confidence in me, the situation could have been very unpleasant. The suggestions of Jesus in Matthew 17 could have nipped this problem in the bud. They are very practical, but it takes courage to implement them.

I have not always seen the importance of bridling the tongue. Indeed, I regret to say, in seminary one of my favorite indoor pastimes was picking apart other seminarians, professors and high-placed clerics. This kind of action seemed to prevail as a general entertainment. No one suggested that it wasn't exactly the Christian way. As I went into my first parish, I continued the practice. It seemed to give me a sense of wisdom and superiority to be able to uncover and dissect the moral tumors of others, particularly successful clergy in the diocese.

I well remember my moment of enlightenment in this matter. I had performed a wedding and was in the process of taking some of the flowers out to the reception at the bride's home. Helping me was a member of the altar guild who told me that she had been reading a publication I had never viewed with high theological regard. Somehow the conversation turned to gossip and my friend said, "I have learned from my religious magazine that I have no right to speak negatively or judgingly about any other human being." I was shaken, for I knew instantly that she was right and that her information was right in this matter. Gossip usually proceeds out of sheer maliciousness, arrogance, cowardice, lack of self-esteem and pride. It may well be a worse breach of the law than a sin of the flesh such as adultery, which sometimes has a grain of love within it.

From that day on I have tried to keep my negative criticism to myself. I have often failed, but then I get up again without flailing myself with remorse and try again. As pastor in one congregation for twenty years, I came to realize that there can be no real growth in love toward any specific person, or growth in love in general, until we cease talking cruelly about other people. I describe the dangers of this practice in a pamphlet, *Gossip*. Doing unkindnesses and saying them create a climate in which love does not grow.[9]

Teresa of Avila speaks of the vital importance of this rule for all on the religious way:

> But the safe path for the soul that practices prayer will be not to bother about anything or anyone and to pay attention

to itself and to pleasing God. This is important — ah, if I should have to speak of the mistakes I have seen happen by trusting in good intentions! But let us strive always to look at virtues and good deeds we see in others and cover their defects with the thought of our own great sins. This is a manner of acting that, although we cannot do so with perfection right away, gradually gains for us a great virtue, that is: considering all others better than ourselves.[10]

Praying for the Enemy

In the fifth step we move from the practices we need to *cease* doing and turn toward actions we need to *do* to encourage love of enemies. I find that praying for the people whom I dislike and the ones who dislike me has both a practical and religious effect. In my journal I keep a list of people for whom I pray. I have listed there those who are particularly important to me, those who are sick, those who have asked for prayer, *and those who might be called enemies.* I scatter these people with whom I have trouble all throughout the list, so if my prayer list falls into others' hands, they will be no wiser.

The best method of praying in a general way for other people is to pray the Lord's Prayer for them. If John is the one I am praying for, I pray: "John's Father who art in heaven, Hallowed be thy name in John, Thy kingdom come in John, Thy will be done in John, on earth just as if he were with you in heaven. Give him his daily bread, all that he needs to sustain and enrich his life. Forgive John and help him to forgive others. Do not put John to the test as he is weak like the rest of us, and please deliver John from the Evil One. Let John's joy be in your kingdom and power and glory forever and ever." While I am praying in this way, I visualize John and imagine the risen Christ with him.

Praying like this for the enemy has several practical effects. If I am asking God to take care of several people and to pour blessings upon them, this impedes me from saying or doing anything unkind to them. Such negative action would be at odds with what I am asking God to do and would make me a sheer hypocrite. It would put me in the position of saying, "Lord, you take care of John eternally, while I'll fix him here below."

There is also a real power in intercession. For some people it can be their primary vocation. We human beings are in much closer contact with one another than we have been taught to believe by our materialistic culture. The study of parapsychology shows that we have non-sensory ways of reaching out to other people. The Dean of the Engineering School at Princeton sponsored a study of telepathy and energy with one of his students and published the material in the *Princeton Alumni Weekly*.[11] When we deny that our psyches are strangely interrelated, we are closing our minds to observable facts which have been replicated in laboratories all over the world. Thus, when we are praying for someone earnestly, imaginatively, something often gets through; space and time do not seem to make much difference. (Unfortunately, hatred and malice when meditated upon can also get through; this is the basis of truth in witchcraft.) Real prayer opens one to a new dimension of reality and can be a channel for the healing love of God.

When I first considered the possible effectiveness of intercession, I decided to take on a difficult project. I picked a woman in the parish who was nasty, cantankerous, gossipy and domineering. Most of the people in the church were afraid of her, and her family was terrorized by her. If prayer could help Ethel, I was sure it could help anyone. I began praying for her daily, often using the method which I suggest above. About three weeks later I received a call from Ethel. She wanted to come and see me. In fear and trembling I made the appointment, wondering what kind of trouble was brewing. When she came into my office, she flopped down in a chair opposite me and began to cry. She said that she realized what a horrible person she was, but that she just wanted us at the church to know how much the church meant to her and how much worse she would have been without the influence of the clergy and the church upon her life. I realized that she suffered as much being herself as I did being me. From that time we became good friends, and I realized again the truth that in the depth of us we all carry heavy burdens.

Positive Action

If my attempt to love the enemy ceases with prayer, love will probably not come to fruition. We need prayer *and action*. My sixth suggestion, therefore, consists of examining the life of the one whom we do not love (or like) and looking long and hard enough to find something positive and creative in that person, something we can genuinely admire. I have discovered that with real effort we can find something admirable in everyone. With some people, I'll admit, it takes much longer, but there are redeeming qualities in everyone.

And then, when the opportunity comes, we can simply make the positive observation we have discovered. The effects of such an action can be quite surprising. I remember being in a group of one of the guilds at the church, and the tongues were sharpened for moral dissection. The former president of the guild was on the table for an exploratory moral operation. The list of this person's failings grew and grew until someone remarked, "But did you ever notice what a fine job she has done as a widow in raising her son?" It was like a bombshell. The whole tone of the group changed, and the conversation about the woman ceased.

Attorneys tell me that it is difficult for them to defend most clients without coming to have a higher regard for them. It is nearly impossible to become another's defender and protector without having our appreciation for that person increase. When we know a lot about another, we realize that all of us are having a hard struggle. This generates at least pity, and pity is close to compassion, and this is not far from love. A ninth-century Islamic mystic, Sai-al-Sakadi, put it so well: "Perfect love exists between two people only when each addresses the other with the words, 'O, myself!' "; we are one in our faults.

In his novel, *The Heart of the Matter*, Graham Greene's main character, Major Scobie, is profoundly aware of the poignancy of everyone's story when one gets to know the story well; Scobie is a policeman, and so he digs up lots of *facts* about people — and the more facts, the more pity (the more you know, the less you can stereotype and judge). In this scene, he's helping out at the site of a disaster at sea (the setting of the novel is Africa during World War II); outside everything looks placid, but in the rest-house, he knows, there are wounded people:

> Outside the rest-house he stopped again. The lights inside would have given an extraordinary impression of peace if one hadn't known, just as the stars on this clear night gave also an impression of remoteness, security, freedom. If one knew, he wondered, the facts, would one have to feel pity even for the planets? if one reached what they called the heart of the matter?[12]

Active Kindness

The seventh and last suggestion is like the sixth. Let us try to perform some kind act for the persons whom we are trying to love, something that will make them happy. We can watch the individuals, see what would give them joy, and then perform the action, give the gift, provide the positive situation for those people without having them even know that we had anything to do with it. The effect is often miraculous. It is very difficult, if not impossible, to dislike persons whom we have made happy. It is almost inhuman not to rejoice with others when we have brought them joy. Our gift may be either some small act of consideration or something which requires greater effort, but it makes no difference as long as our action brings happiness to the person. Whenever joy is expressed by others, of course, they become more lovable, too.

In the final analysis, it is not the people who do things for us that we love the most, but the people for whom we do things. This is a fundamental psychological law. When others do something for us, it often causes us to feel obligated. When we do something for others without any expectations, we are closely in tune with the central core of reality and are sustained and strengthened by love.

The love we feel for our children exemplifies this truth. We have done so much for them, partly because we had to so that they could survive, partly because we wanted to, and also partly because they needed what we had to give. We share our lives with our children, and in sharing them we participate in love itself. This kind of giving of ourselves works outside the family group as well as within it. If we try it, we may well find that our specific dislikes can turn into love.

As our love begins to grow and increase toward those who have been our enemies, we begin to realize more and more fully the importance and power of love and our need for it.

Someone asked me once what happens when we have dealt with all the enemies in our lives. I replied that we need not worry. God loves us so much and is so interested in our growth that in his infinite mercy and love, he will always provide us with a few more.[13]

Caring for the Stranger

When we discuss the Christian mandate to love the stranger, the first question to answer is: "Who is the stranger?" As I have already noted, we live in a global world. There are strangers whom we meet daily and there are strangers whom we know only through the media — those from all over the world whom we read about or see as we switch on the television. The problems that face our world are staggering. Are we loving one another as Jesus loved us if we ignore these problems? Should not our concern reach out to both the strangers in church and those throughout the world? In the story that Jesus told about Lazarus lying sick and hungry at the rich man's door, Jesus was not condemning wealth in itself. Rather, Jesus condemned the rich man because he *ignored* the plight of the man lying at his door whom his servants could have fed with the scraps from his table.

Without any great trouble, his servants could have provided a mat, some clothes and even a shelter near the stable. The name of the rich man has disappeared like a wisp of smoke, but Lazarus' name has lived on for nearly two thousand years — and interestingly, this story in the New Testament follows a few verses after the stories of the loving father with two sons and the dishonest manager, stories of the unconditional love of God.

Strangers Near and Far Away

As we look beyond our circle of friends and family, out beyond our neighborhood and our acquaintances, beyond our business associates and our enemies, we find the stranger, the unknown person whom we pass by on the street. Other strangers we know only through imagination and news reports. Unless we extend ourselves for the strangers who daily cross our paths, our efforts toward those whom we do not know will be only hollow and artificial.

After suggesting some ways to care for the strangers around us, I will look at world problems: How can we learn to protect our fragile blue planet so that it may nourish and sustain its growing population of human beings? How do we reach out to relieve poverty, sickness and misery in our own country and all over the world? How do we eliminate the incredible misery and destruction caused by the curse of war? How do we share our concern by providing education that enables people to help and love themselves and one another? We need to be aware of all of these conditions; they are of the greatest importance for us and our grandchildren and their grandchildren. Indeed, Christian love that does not reach out into the world is hardly love at all.

Then there is the question of our giving, which can do much to implement our care and concern for others. This is equally important for all of us, particularly for us who are unable to be active except by giving of our substance. If we give generously and with love, it can be a true expression of concern for the stranger — so long as we remember that it is the love that counts.

Paul reminds us that without love, giving away everything we have is of little value. Certainly we who do not give generously of our substance and do not reach out as we are able to heal our broken world have never caught the full implications of love for the unknown and the forgotten, for the stranger. So much seems to be demanded of us by Jesus' injunction to "love one another as I have loved you."

We Need One Another

In our atomized society, few people live long in the same community. The sense of social solidarity has broken down, and we have become more and more strangers to one another. There is no place where this problem is more clear than on our large college campuses. One college leader told me that in no place in human history have greater numbers of unrelated human beings been brought together in one spot than on the modern large state university campus. And in no place is there greater loneliness.

Several years ago a suicide occurred on the University of Notre Dame campus. This is unusual for a Catholic college, whose students have been taught that suicide is not an acceptable way of exiting from this world. It is even more unusual at Notre Dame, where there are excellent dormitories supervised by priests, nuns, religious brothers or trained laypeople in residence in each of them. Notre Dame's Director of Student Affairs was troubled and decided to get at the cause of this tragedy. He called in all the students who had attended classes with the unfortunate student and also interviewed those who lived up and down the hall in the dormitory where the student had lived. He wanted to know what kind of person this student was. What he discovered was that *no one even knew him*. It is little wonder that the young man took his life.

Simply being around other people does not mean that we are escaping loneliness. The worst and most poignant loneliness is found in the rooming-house districts of great cities where swarms of people live but have no fellowship — no meeting of person with person. Most of these people have nothing to do, and this usually leads to boredom and hopelessness.

Another place where one finds great loneliness is among the very wealthy. Many of them have found that most of the people who seek them out want only to share in their wealth. Thus, these wealthy people feel used rather than related to. It is not physical pain that brings the greatest misery, but psychic pain. Loneliness, alienation and the sense of being a stranger to others are often a part of destructive psychic pain.

Some people are lonely even in the midst of families. They have not been made to feel that they have value just as they are. They feel rejected and believe that no one truly cares for them. All human relationship seems a mockery to them. In the best of psychological and spiritual counseling, one of the goals is to break down the barriers of loneliness. Then we may meet and care for one another, offering and receiving fresh air for this staleness of the soul.

Many people become disturbed at holiday seasons, especially Christmas. They look back into their childhoods and remember that at this one time mercy and love seemed to flow naturally and freely. As Christmas approaches they look forward with anticipation, hoping that they may capture the same spirit once again. When the miracle does not happen, then their hopes and expectations crash in upon them, and they realize what alienated strangers they are. They crumble into the Christmas neurosis, in the unbearable reality of their loneliness.

Seeing Strangers

One does not have to be a professional psychologist in order to reach out to the stranger. All of us can do something. First of all, reaching out to the stranger has to have a high priority on our list of activities. We need to realize how life-giving this kind of action can be.

One of the finest tributes I heard about my mother after her death came from a peddler. When he stopped by and found that she had died, he told me that my mother had always welcomed him, had him sit down on the porch and then brought him a cool drink. They would talk for a while, and perhaps she would buy a few trifles. The man told me that this refreshed him and gave him a sense of being part of the human race once again.

For several years I conducted classes at Notre Dame in a course entitled, "Personal Perspectives in Nonviolence." The director of the Nonviolence Program developed the course because he had come to realize that many of the students came into the program for violent reasons and that before they could legitimately work in situations of outer violence, they had to deal with their own inner violence. The class met in small groups of no more than fifteen. Sometimes I would come into the first class, explain the course and then be silent. Often the silence would continue for a half hour or longer before the students could overcome their fear of one another and the professor and begin a discussion. So many of us wonder if anyone else really wants anything to do with us, often our violence springs out of this fear. Someone has remarked that human beings have this in common with dogs — strangeness intimidates and enrages them. We seldom stop to think how alien we feel and how much we need each other.

The second step, then, in reaching out to strangers is the same step we need to take in any spiritual undertaking: We need to stop our busyness and be still. Then we remember that we are loved unconditionally by the Creator and belong to the same human family. The third step is to mobilize our will to reach out to another to give as we have been given to. The fourth step is to realize that we feel alien, and yet that we are not alone. With divine Love with us, who can be against us? The fifth step is to *look out and see the stranger.* This may appear quite simple to do, but it is not as simple as it sounds. In order to see the stranger, we must be aware enough to look beyond ourselves.

We need to be quiet and be conscious enough so that we are not thinking only of ourselves, our family and our circle, our clique, our reactions, our desires. It is difficult for us to be truly aware of the world around us and particularly of the people around us. We usually live with habitual perceptions and according to established patterns. Frequently when we are in a group, we gravitate immediately to our own friends and start talking about the latest thing of common interest in our circle.

So Many Needy Strangers

We seldom pause in a group and look around and say to ourselves: "I wonder if there is someone here who is new or lonely, a person who needs my friendship." Having been strangers in a strange land, as the Hebrews were in Egypt, can open us up to the pain of being a stranger. Although I have often felt inwardly uncomfortable in my native country, separated and different, once I was outwardly a stranger as well. I was in Switzerland for a long stay. My passport was taken from me because the Swiss government wanted to make sure I did not earn any money in their country without paying taxes. I was an *alien*. I was not a citizen. I did not know my rights. I was a stranger. When the plane home landed in Los Angeles, I wanted to get down and kiss the ground. I was home; I was no longer a stranger. Similarly, the worst thing about being in prison is that prisoners have lost their rights; they have become strangers. The forgotten, the sick, the hungry feel the same way.

We do not like to be aware of the fact that we are often strangers in the midst of strangers. Have you ever noticed what happens when a group of strangers get into an elevator? We treat each other like *strangers*. We don't look at each other. It often seems that there must be a law prohibiting speech in elevators. The silence is oppressive, and we are almost glad when we can get off at our floor.

Unfortunately, churches are often no more friendly than elevators, particularly large churches. When my wife and I first went to the Cathedral in Phoenix, Arizona, we tried an experiment. I was the new canon at the Cathedral. Barbara did not announce that she was the canon's wife, and she quietly attended the early service every Sunday morning for two months before anyone spoke to her, a stranger. In many churches the gospel statement, "Many are called, but few are chosen," could well be parodied: "Many are cold, but few are frozen." One can often find as much fellowship by going to a theater as by going to church.

Some people do not like to pass the peace at eucharist, and yet this is one of the most ancient and integral parts of eucharist. It is an attempt to realize our common bond with one another. If, however, the peace does not move outside the church into an easy conversation, it is not genuine. The peace should be a symbol of loving care which continues on after the services.

I can understand why people were uncomfortable receiving Communion during the Middle Ages. Knowing that the body and blood of the loving Christ was coursing through their veins and yet sensing no change in themselves, medieval people began to feel guilty. Perhaps we should feel guilty as well. What is our spiritual state if we exchange the peace and receive eucharist, and then do not greet the same people as we leave the church or meet them later in the street? We are not reaching out to strangers.

Most of the evil in this world is caused not by wicked people but by unconscious people, by the very kind of unconsciousness which lets us ignore others. Unconscious people are run not by conscious motivation but rather by whatever pops up out of their unconscious depths. Sometimes it is an action of thoughtfulness or forgiveness, but it can just as well be impulsiveness, annoyance, a bigoted cultural heritage, a stupid prejudice, indifference or fear. It takes real discipline to be genuinely evil, as Charles Williams points out so clearly in his novel, *Shadows of Ecstasy*. But the easiest thing in the world is to live unconsciously. In a letter to a priest friend, Jung states that perhaps the essence of most evil and sin is unconsciousness.

A friend of mine returning from World War II told me of an experience that showed him how his prejudices made others strangers to him. In the South Pacific he met and became fast friends with a soldier about his own age. After the war they arranged to meet again below the clock at Grand Central Station in New York. He saw a man approaching him wearing a ghastly green suit. It was his friend. The realization suddenly struck him that if he had not met his friend in the service, where they were wearing the same G.I. garb, his prejudice about clothes would have kept him from his closest friendship. He never would have given the time of day to anyone dressed like this. We often wear blinders that keep us from true sight.

Reaching Out

Being aware of strangers requires some growth in consciousness. Seldom is this achieved without reflection and prayer. This is another example of how loving action is seldom possible unless it is rooted in prayer. As I pray, some more scales fall from my eyes, and I see that other persons or groups of people are just as frightened and alien as I am. I see their hungry eyes, their eager expectancy. Of course, I may not be reading the situation correctly, but I will never know unless I take the next step and reach out with an extended hand or a word of greeting to the person whom I have seen only as a stranger.

This is difficult for an introvert, just as difficult as it is for an extrovert to take time in quiet and reflection. But it helps to remember that even if the other person doesn't want to be reached out to, our attempt to reach out can do no harm as long as we have no hidden expectations and are truly more interested in understanding than in being understood.

What do we say as we make the first approach to a stranger? I have found that three questions unlock conversation after we have introduced ourselves: Where are you from? What do you do for a living? Do you have a family? If people are traveling, they nearly always like to talk about home. If they are newcomers, they like to tell of where they have been. Sometimes we can talk about places we have both been. If we hit upon an oldtimer in the community, he or she can regale us with family history. I love to talk about where I have been and where I was raised, because I am talking about myself with someone who seems interested.

It is painful to realize how seldom people ask us what we are doing and why. I have learned a great deal by asking people why they happen to be at the place where I meet them. Seldom do we get an opportunity to tell other people about the dull or even the interesting details of our ordinary lives. Here again we can share experiences, and as we do, we are less strangers to one another. Again, I love to be asked about my multifaceted life and to tell about the various things I do.

If we are alone and separated from our family, most of us enjoy telling about them. If they are with us, this gives us an opportunity for introductions. If our children are grown, we can tell of their lives and successes. Often pictures will come out and barriers begin to crumble. I always carry pictures of my extended family with me. When a person is interested enough in me to ask about my family, it is a pleasure to pull the pictures out and share them.

These three questions lead into a dozen others, and before very long we are no longer strangers. It is as if our two frightened little inner children have learned to play with each other and have become divine children. When friendship really begins to grow, we may even talk about our inner problems; then we find that the world is not as terrifying and hostile and strange a place as we had feared. Other people, we discover, are much like us.

Quite obviously we can't shepherd every stranger that we meet. We cannot call upon all the shut-ins and the sick in our community. We cannot visit everyone who is in prison. We need time for reflection to find out which ones belong to us and are part of our bundle, which situations have our names on them. We may find that our task is not so much reaching out to others ourselves as organizing people who wish to meet the strangers, who wish to minister to the hungry, who want to call on the sick and the lonely, to visit prisoners, to greet strangers. This ministry is part of the priesthood of all true believers.

I have given many dozen conferences during the last thirty-five years. Those seminars that provided fellowship groups where people can share their life stories have been most effective. Of course, confidentiality must be a part of such sharing.

A Christian church which is not organized to reach out to the strangers in its midst is simply not living out the gospel message. Every church, therefore, needs to develop a lay ministry of outreach to the strangers within it and around it. Each church also needs social groups into which strangers can be integrated. Most churches need to provide an opportunity for fellowship; ongoing fellowship is a part of genuine Christian worship.

But we must bear in mind that surface friendliness which does not genuinely go out to others can be quite harmful. It is almost worse to be greeted and welcomed one day and ignored the next week than to have been left alone in the first place. I need to back up my outreach to the stranger with action — an invitation to dinner, to have a cup of coffee, to meet some friends of mine who have a common interest, to play a game of bridge, to come to a church group. *It is important that we do not promise more than we can deliver.* Reaching all the strangers who need our care requires more than individual effort; it requires structures to reach out and integrate those who wish it.

A wise counselor gave me one last word of caution in dealing with strangers. When strangers have the courage to call on us, it usually means that they are in real need, and we should make every effort to see them soon. When a stranger leaps over the barriers of separateness and asks for help, it usually indicates genuine problems. We may not be able to handle the problem, but we can listen and then find someone who can truly help. The cry from a stranger is usually an urgent cry. We need to take time for it even if it costs us dearly.

This Fragile Earth, Our Island Home

For most of its time on earth, the species from which we humans sprang was a relatively insignificant part of earth's fauna. And then several million years ago the brain of one branch of the primates went into a gigantic mutation. The Creator brought forth a new kind of creature on the face of the earth: one who could think, reflect, love, play, seek power; one with religious insights and experiences; a myth-making and artistic living being.

Slowly a great matrilineal culture began to grow up, and then this several hundred-thousand-year-old culture was displaced only six thousand years ago as patriarchy developed and made power and domination the central features of human society. The empires of Egypt and Babylon and along the Indus River and in China flourished through the power of the sword, and "civilization" was born. The leaders placated the gods to guard against earthquake, tidal waves and other disasters, but they cared little for the earth, unlike those in former times who had lived in closer touch with it. Many species of animals were destroyed as a result of this power hunger, and they disappeared forever. Nations and empires battled for each other's wealth and power; human beings became one of the few species that systematically destroys its own kind.

Even humans warring on each other have not slowed the population growth. George Howard, chair of the psychology department at the University of Notre Dame, has written these alarming words about the graph of world population:

> The line creeps along low, almost flat, for centuries. Around A.D. 1000 it begins to rise slowly. Then in the 10th century something startling happens: It shoots straight up. The line graphs human population over time, and it says we're headed for trouble. With a capital T.
>
> It took millions of years for the world's population to increase from a mere handful to a crowd of one billion. Adding the second billion took only 117 years; 33 years were required to accumulate the third; 14 years produced the fourth and 13 years the fifth. The sixth billion is due on board later this decade.... If unchecked, human population growth will inevitably produce an array of crises throughout the 21st century.[14]

Loving one another is no longer an option; it has become a necessity for the survival of human beings in the years ahead.

As the years passed, secular Western civilization grew up totally cut off from value or meaning or religious ideas. Wars became fiercer and fiercer. Finally our species learned how to unlock the secrets of matter; we discovered that enormous energy, unimaginable power, lay locked in what appeared to be inert matter — and then the atomic bomb became a reality and nuclear warfare an ominous possibility. Before the bomb was first tested, scientists feared that it might cause a chain reaction and destroy our whole world — and yet we foolish humans took the risk and tested it anyway. Indeed, we still don't know how many nuclear blasts might trigger the utter destruction of the earth and all living creatures on it.

Our Fragile Earth

As human beings have learned to control their environment and to protect themselves from disease, they have proliferated all over the earth. They have cut down the great forests that once covered much of the earth's surface, forests that poured oxygen into the atmosphere. Rivers and lakes and even oceans have been polluted. Land devoid of vegetation has eroded away and become desert. We humans have even poisoned the atmosphere as we have continued to burn fossil fuels and pour other wastes into the sky. I was brought up in a town set in a beautiful gap where a river passed through a mountain range. But large chemical plants were built there, and over the years they belched poisonous gases into the air. Recently I returned to this town and found what looked like a moonscape rather than the verdant mountains I knew as a child.

This earth of ours is indeed fragile; it can be destroyed. We are not loving our neighbor or grandchildren unless we use our best wisdom and effort to care for this earth — created so human beings could emerge to learn the mystery of LOVE — to receive it and share it.

Human beings are part of this physical world in which we live. Some of us live in physical comfort, free from disease, protected from other human beings by great war machines and by national boundaries that are like gigantic glaciers that cut people off from one another. However, a large percentage of men, women and children live in poverty and under oppression; many do not have enough to eat, are wracked by disease and live in subhuman conditions. Their life expectancies are half or less than those of the people who live in more humane surroundings. We are not loving our neighbors when some human beings prosper and others starve and die. Some human linguistic and ethnic groups are endangered species, much like many animals and birds and reptiles. If human beings are to survive, we need to learn how to love one another and work together with other human beings with understanding, consolation and love. Selfishness, greed, domination, oppression, fear, hatred and war could wipe the earth clean of the whole human race.

Taking Care of Our Bodies

Many of us have a tendency to take our bodies for granted. We want to live long and free from illness, but we don't think much further than that. We forget that our bodies are the one part of the total environment over which we have a great amount of control; often we ignore our responsibility to the most personal portion of the physical world, our own bodies.

These bodies of ours are God's amazingly intricate creation; if we mistreat them, we can destroy or weaken them. Paul said that the body is the temple of the Holy Spirit. But do we treat our bodies with the same kind of respect that we would show toward the holy of holies within the temple? How do we feed our bodies, exercise them, rest them, give them companionship, clean them, relax them, listen to them, enjoy and love them, care for them?

In some religious groups (even among Christians), the body has been seen as a deterrent to true religion. Suffering, penance, ascetic practices, rejection, denial of legitimate needs and actual abuse of the body have been suggested as ways of advancing along the religious way. Of course, the body and its pleasure can become the total preoccupation for some people, but this happens only when the body is idolized, made an end in itself. How many of us really treat our bodies well — as well as we do a plant or an animal that we love? These bodies of ours are very tough and very fragile; just like the rest of our island home, they need our wise, tender, loving care. Our lives can hardly achieve our deepest expression of love in a body that has been neglected, ignored, mistreated or abused.

And these bodies respond not only to our conscious care but also to our emotional and religious life. Fear, anger, depression and stress — and excessive egocentricity — cause immeasurable damage to our physical health. The body of a person without hope, love and meaning often is sick and sometimes dies. And when we die, the world loses a possible source of love.

We can hardly deal adequately with the spiritual domain if we do not come to know our physical world and treat it with respect and love. This means that we need to become mature as persons, treating ourselves and others with understanding; we need to know the wonders and dangers of our fragile island home, of which our bodies are a part. We need to use our material substance sacramentally. In this way we prepare to experience the kingdom of love, now and always.

Money, Mammon and Addiction

Money is a very touchy subject, but it is a reality that is always with us. We no longer have a barter system; our incredibly complex society runs on money. In order to survive in our society, most of us have to learn to do some task that is valued enough by society to give us (and, if we are married, to give our families) enough money to live on, enough to carry us through the crises that most people face at times, enough to see that our children are educated.

But how much money is enough? Unfortunately, many of us can become addicted to money. This addiction can be more dangerous than addictions to heroin or alcohol; drugs affect only a few, while wealth addiction gives one person power over others and can drive the addict to take from the poor the little they have. One of the strange characteristics of wealth addicts is that they seldom enjoy their money, as Philip Slater points out in his provocative book, *Wealth Addiction*. Whenever any one aspect of life becomes the total focus of our energy — our single goal — our lives go out of kilter, and what we pursue can become demonic. In fact, single-minded concentration even on one spiritual gift can be as corrupting as any addiction within the material world — whether it be to sex, approval, drugs, power or wealth. Real love is balanced. (Addiction to power and wealth, by the way, are intertwined.)

One of the finest outreaches of the pioneering Church of the Savior in Washington, D.C. is the Ministry of Money.[15] This church organizes trips to some of the poorest sections of the planet, enabling affluent Americans to find that they can be ministered to by the poor and that their money can alleviate the anguish of the hungry and broken people of the world. People grow as they minister with love and money to less fortunate human beings — it is so important to learn the creative use of money.

It is nearly impossible to remain in contact with the realm of the spirit unless we give some of our material substance for religious and charitable purposes, although we need, of course, to be careful to fund groups that share our gifts wisely. It is nonsense to maintain that we want to have access to the realm of Spirit with its love and power, that we are giving ourselves with utter sincerity to God, if we spend all but a tiny fraction of our financial resources on ourselves, on our own desires and interests, or on the quest for more money. To say that we are truly committed and still to remain in such a selfish frame of mind is worse than nonsense: It is hypocrisy. And Jesus did not have much truck with hypocrites. For those who do not give of their substance, the spiritual realm usually closes and remains closed, except for occasional flashes of lightning. Money is our congealed energy and being, what the world gives us for what it thinks we are worth.[16] Sharing our wealth is a form of love if it is given in love and with love.

Concern for Others in the Lord's Prayer

Should we doubt that we are called to reach out to others, we need only turn to the Lord's Prayer for confirmation of this conviction. Jesus taught his disciples this prayer, and it contains the essence of his belief and practice. Within the rhythmic words of this prayer there is the insistent beat of concern for others, again and again. It is almost impossible to say this prayer without realizing that we are being asked to pray with the whole human race as our family. We cannot isolate ourselves and truly pray these words.

First of all, I do not pray to my Father, but to *our* Father. As I turn to the loving Father, to *Abba*, I bring not only myself and those dearest to me, but I bring with me all my brothers and sisters from all over the world — black, red, yellow and white, rich and poor, enslaved and free.

I do not ask to enter a solitary, isolated communion with the Father, but rather I ask for *the kingdom*, for a fellowship in which all humanity is joined in harmony, concern and love empowered by the love of Abba.

I do not ask that this kingdom be given just to me or my family or my community or my church or my nation, but that it may come to *all the earth* as it is given in heaven.

I petition not for my daily bread, for my daily sustenance of body, mind and soul, but for *our* daily need; I ask that all the human family may be fed and sheltered and given psychological nourishment and spiritual direction. Again, this prayer must be backed up by specific action on my part or I run the danger of falling into hypocrisy.

When asking for forgiveness, it is the same: "Forgive *us our* trespasses as *we* forgive those who trespass against *us*." How different it would be if I asked: "Forgive me my trespasses as I forgive those who trespass against me." Often the hurts which are most difficult to forgive are done not to me but to those I love. In this prayer, then, we are praying that forgiveness may grow among us all. So it is difficult to sincerely pray this prayer while we harbor malice toward others in our hearts.

The beat becomes almost monotonous. Father, *we* are weak and fragile human beings, *all of us*, and do not put *us* to the test, or allow *us* to be led into temptation, but save *us* from the day of trial. We are all in this together.

And, Father, we know that, try as hard as we can, *we cannot save ourselves* from the forces of evil, from the Evil One. Only as you share your kingdom and power and glory with us can we have the strength not to be swept away into the abyss. Father, protect and deliver *all of us*, your children, from all evil.

It is nearly impossible to say this prayer, let alone to truly *pray* it, without realizing that we are all one family. I cannot ask this loving Father anything for myself without asking for others as well. My prayer is likely to be hollow and empty unless this truth is expressed by me in some kind of action for the miserable ones next door and all over the earth.

The Invincible Power of Love

Part I: A Recovered Childhood

Our memories are spotty at best and quite selective as well. In addition, the first three or four years are lost in hidden recesses of the developing brain and mind. They are largely lost unless we are told about them. If we have had younger siblings and have seen how they were treated, we can infer that our childhood was much like theirs. However, I was the younger of two children. I knew few other children younger than I, and I never played with them. I was never near a baby, and never held one in my arms. My memory of the first four years of my life has been a blank slate. It was many years before I realized how crucial these years are in human development, and I was in my middle seventies when I realized my own childhood was a mystery to me.

By then it was hard to find anyone who would remember stories of my early life: I was the youngest child of a youngest child, and all of my relatives were dead —mother, father, brother and cousins. I knew of no one who could tell me of the hidden years. Worse yet, most of the childhood memories I did have were very unpleasant. When I told Barbara Hannah, the well-known Jungian analyst in Zurich, about what I remembered of sickness and rejection, she exclaimed: "Your parents gave you just enough love to keep you alive." Both of my parents were classic Victorians. Babies were still brought by storks. My mother could no more tell me about my birth than she could have described the intimate details of her love life. I doubt if my father was present at my birth, but if he had been, it would have been as impossible for him to speak of it as it was for my mother. My paternal grandfather was born in 1830, and my father was reared in pure Victorian.

Through the years I gleaned a few facts about my childhood. I was a blue baby born in a zinc-smelting town in rural Illinois. My cradle had been a very large shoe box placed on the open oven door of a coal stove in the kitchen. At six months of age my mother carried me in a cradle-basket to Palmerton, Pennsylvania, where my father was to be the manager of the company in a company town. This was the same cradle that all three of our children slept in many years later, and my wife, Barbara, could not believe that I slept in that portable cradle at six months; all three of our children had outgrown it after six weeks.

As I grew older, I asked about a ridge at the back of my head and was told that this was caused by the forceps that crushed my head at birth. Only in college did I realize that I was nearly deaf and that this was the reason my speech was unclear; in order to survive as a child I had spontaneously learned to read lips. Two years of intensive speech therapy remedied the unclear speaking. (This was sixty years ago, when little was known about hearing loss and few effective hearing aids were available.) Because of my slurred speech and a mild cerebral palsy that often causes exaggerated emotion, my parents did not think I was quite bright or able to cope with the world. Many years later, when I visited an aunt, she showed me a letter written at the time of my birth from one grandmother to the other, lamenting: "How tragic that Myra and Maynard [my parents] have been burdened by such a hopelessly damaged and deformed child."

My mother taught me first grade at home using the Calvert system, fearing I could not manage school. The next year I entered the local school, and in third grade I was given a routine Stanford-Binet intelligence test. They were so surprised at the results that they gave it to me a second time. I remember that incident; I viewed the test as a delightful game.

Later my mother confided in me that before the Stanford-Binet they had been advised to find a home for retarded children, as I would always be a burden to them. My parents' advice from their family doctor was that there was little hope or future for me. The meaning of my mother's cryptic remark to me (to which I referred to in the first chapter—that it would have served her right if I had rejected her) during her extended fatal illness became quite clear to me. She had not paid much attention to me and had concentrated her efforts on my father and brother, and on her "job" as manager's wife. I had been considered a hopeless case.

Ninety years ago, Palmerton was a new factory town in rural Pennsylvania, a hundred miles from New York and ninety miles from Philadelphia, in the heart of the Pennsylvania Dutch country. My mother was expected to see that the new wives of the managerial staff were integrated into the life of this new town. The company had a large and highly developed research division; most of these men and their wives were highly educated and had little in common with the workers, who had come directly from the Balkans, or with the local people, who had few educational advantages. My mother had a busy life calling on new company families and hosting luncheons and dinner parties each week. One of her children now went to school, but she had to have some sitters to take care of me. Years later I remembered the constant flow of these sitters, but remember the name of only one of them, Stephena Partel.

One of the happiest memories of an otherwise bleak childhood were the Seneca legends my mother told my friends and me from memory. We were all spellbound as she related the adventures of these Seneca heroes. They lived in a world where the supernatural and spiritual surrounded and penetrated the physical world of forest and rivers, of corn and game. In their world, good always won in the end. My mother knew these stories because as a young girl, she had gone with her father, a Presbyterian missionary to the Senecas, as he visited these remarkable people. She grew close to many of the children; she was adopted into one of their clans. As a college student she wanted to record these myths, and the old storytellers were delighted to tell them to her. Grandfather's Seneca interpreter translated the stories as she took them down by hand in a notebook that I still have. These stories presented the spiritual world as very close and benign. They were an exciting introduction to religion.

I had always thought of these stories as children's stories. But years later my editor pointed out to me that these stories are hero myths similar to the myths of many other cultures. As I studied them, I found that the same religious symbols are present among all people. The deepest levels of these stories were similar to the great symbols of Christianity. I collected the stories in the book *Dreamquest: Native American Myth and Recovery of Soul*, an exploration of Seneca life. I showed how these stories could only be understood when we knew the creation myth of this people. I went on to tell, in this book, how we made an annual trek from Eastern Pennsylvania to Western New York State in our open Buick touring car. The trip was a delightful adventure and took two days — and we stayed in a real hotel. My mother was the driver; my father almost never came with us. These trips went so far back in my memory that I thought that they had always been taking place.

These details may seem irrelevant, but they usher in a story of unceasing love. During the Christmas season of 1993, I received a strange letter that had been mailed in Palmerton. I did not recognize the name on the return sticker, Clara Smith Kleintop, a common name among the Pennsylvania Dutch. The writer asked if I was still alive (I was seventy-seven at the time) and if I was still writing books. Clara then mentioned that she had taken care of me as a child. But Clara's name still did not ring a bell.

However, I decided to write to her immediately. At the time it did not occur to me how old she must have been. In order to show her I was still alive and writing, I sent her a copy of my latest book, *Dreamquest*. Within two weeks I received a letter in return. I could have sent her no better book. She wrote: "I remember very well those long trips to Salamanca on the Seneca Reservation. *I was holding you during those long trips in the Buick touring car.*" What she described told me that she had cared for me during the lost years of childhood; she had known me very well. At seventy-seven I could still learn about my birth and childhood. She was ninety-one and still active and spry.

Many letters and phone calls took place in the months that

followed. The story of our relationship emerged quickly. She wanted to go to high school and get an education and she lived in the country far from a school. Somehow she and my mother found each other. They made an agreement. She would live in the apartment on the third floor of our home and have her meals as well. She could go to school, and her only responsibility was to care for me and my brother every afternoon and evening and each weekend. My brother required little supervision. For three years I had been the main focus of Clara's love and attention. She then went on to college and graduate school and became a skilled librarian. She had kept track of me through my writing. She had retired years before and had returned to her home town. Clara had married but never had children of her own.

Both my wife and I knew that we had to visit Clara. We needed to be in eastern Pennsylvania, and we settled upon a day when we could meet her at her home and take her out to lunch. Clara and I bonded immediately. I felt that I had always known her, and this feeling grew as the day wore on. My wife and I were late arriving, and we took Clara with us to pick up her friend, Stephena Partel, who had been another of my later childhood caretakers. I remembered Stephena well. She too had worked at our home, and she had also gone to high school. She became a trained nurse and finally received an advanced degree and taught nursing. She was eighty-eight. Stephena produced a picture of me as a child taken seventy-two years before. I was several years older when she took care of me; she would read to me by the hour. She told me that I never wanted her to stop reading and always wanted more. After lunch we dropped Stephena off at her home and then went to spend the rest of the afternoon with Clara.

Clara told me very frankly about my lost childhood. I had not been a Gerber baby. I was tiny even when she took over my care. My skin was the transparent skin of a premature child, and I showed some signs of mild cerebral palsy. I was constantly drooling. Then came the healing words: "But I just loved holding you." Healing words indeed. Her love was not blind; she was only blind to the attitude that she had picked up from my parents

— that I was a hopelessly damaged child. I had found my surrogate mother at seventy-seven. For nearly three years she had watched me grow and develop until even my physical size was normal. Sitting with Clara, something deep within me knew that I had been deeply loved. Something within me felt restored, renewed. I knew that her words were true. For over a thousand days she had been a loving, caring mother whose natural human love may well have given me the tenacity to hope and survive. My wife said it was a religious experience to see us relate; we responded to each other as if our last meeting had been the day before rather than over seventy years before. Before we left, she knew exactly where to find a picture taken of me and her and some of the others who helped at the house. When I told her of my mother's statement about neglecting me, Clara stood up for my mother, remarking that she was a very busy woman with an important job. She then told about visiting the family a few years later (a visit I don't remember); at that time she asked me what subjects I liked best at school, and my mother had replied bluntly: "You don't ask children general questions, only specific ones." Seventy years had not wiped those words from her mind.

Fifteen months have passed since her first letter arrived that restored the years the locust had eaten. Not only did we visit her, but letters and phone calls have kept us in touch. The blank pages of those years have been filled out with technicolor pictures which have given me a vivid image of my childhood and of the love that did so much to heal it. As our relationship became more established, Clara began to fill me in with what she knew about my birth. I had been born five or more weeks premature, and I had been born along with the placenta. She referred to this as being born with a cowl and told me that in folklore such infants were destined for ministry. The doctor whom I had thought had carelessly bungled my delivery had probably saved my life by a quick forceps delivery. I had not known how much skill and caring had been present even in that event.

During our visit I asked Clara how she had happened to write that incredibly illuminating Christmas letter. She said, "I had a hunch, and I followed it." Several months later she admitted that she had tried twice before to communicate with me. I was lecturing in Palmerton, and she was present. She told me how utterly amazed she was to see me talking with ease and clarity to a large group — the child who spoke so unclearly and was wobbly on his feet. After the talk she came up and introduced herself, but apparently her name (if I had really heard it) meant nothing to me, and she did not wish to push herself forward. Being a highly skilled librarian, she had known of some of my writing. After that meeting Clara read one of my books and wrote me an appreciative letter. I had answered it politely, but I did not recognize her name and had no idea of what our relationship had been. But love is patient, and the third time she wrote, I sent her *Dreamquest*. I then discovered that she was the still-living custodian of memories of my childhood.

Only months ago she had some pictures of me copied (she did not wish to give up her own) — another token of genuine love. At ninety-one she was still able to find a seventy-five-year-old snapshot! She included a picture of herself taken when she graduated from high school. Clara, when she first came into my life, was a beautiful, kindly young woman about the age of Mary of Nazareth. I had the picture enlarged; for me it is a symbol of natural divine love, of its patience, its enduring memory, its invincible, healing power.

When I told my daughter about these pictures and what they had meant to me, she asked to see them. She then told me that she had copies of most of them, and she had put together a whole album of my childhood and boyhood pictures. When we broke up my father's home, there was an old box couch nearly filled with snapshots. My family recorded every important event with pictures. Eighty years of snapshots lay there like the jumbled strata of different era rocks. My daughter took all of them as she kept the family records. I had looked often into that couch as a child and youth and never saw those photographs of my childhood. Maybe I did not want to see them or to remember the struggle it took to prod that fearful child into the potential that love had created within him.

We never know the creative effect that genuine love freely given can have on the ultimate direction of our lives. I knew why I had survived. Divine Love provided the love I needed when I had needed it most. I have no idea if there were other applicants for the job, but LOVE and my mother provided the grace that Clara was and still is.

Part II: A Personal and Humbling Lesson in Love

When Clara left our house to go to college, no one filled her place. My memories of childhood do not start until I was five, and most of my memories are not too pleasant. Being the youngest child and having no memories of the Eden-like caring I received from Clara, I knew nothing about the need that little children have for being held, encircled with warmth — loved unconditionally. Once my parents realized that I could think, they gave me rewards for thinking. Because of my lack of coordination, however, I never received kudos for any athletic achievement. Still, in my early teenage years I learned that I could swim like a fish, and I discovered that I had great endurance.

None of this prepared me for parenting. The only model I had for being a father was my own; he, too, had been a youngest child, and he was raised by a faithful but very strict sister twenty years older than he. Through no fault of his own, he knew no more about children than I. My youngest child, John, became my teacher in what children need, and I was a slow learner. Our two older children were raised largely by their mother. When my older son felt that he was not getting enough attention, he went to his mother and asked how he could get more of my time and attention. Barbara had learned and told him: "You go and take hold of your father's sleeve and hang on until he pays attention to you." He did exactly that, and he is now one of my very closest friends. I have already related how I learned of my daughter's need.

John was not that assertive. In addition he was a sensitive

individual; he felt that if one had to ask for love, such love could not be genuine. As long as he was in a fine private school, everything sailed along, but that school folded. Entering fifth grade he was unable to read, and to make things worse the public school was going on half-day sessions. We knew we needed to find a new school, and with the help of a fine child psychologist, we found a school that seemed the right answer to his problems. It was a learning-disability school that had all sorts of children, some of whom were far more disabled than I had been as a child. John wanted to go to a private school, but not that one. But he finally consented.

The school was excellent; the staff immediately gave him a battery of psychological tests. And then I was called in to see the psychologist; I found myself in the unusual position of being on the other side of the table, with the psychologist asking me, "Do you have any idea what this child's problem is?" I replied that I didn't know of any reason other than stubbornness and obstinacy. And then he dropped the bombshell: "The problem with this child is that he doesn't think that you really care for him or love him."

I protested vigorously that whenever I tried to show him love, warmth and affection, he pushed me away. The psychologist continued, "Has it ever occurred to you why he pushes you away? He is testing you to see how much you really do love him."

"At eleven years of age?" I asked.

"Even at eleven," he replied.

We talked for a while. We had a psychological clinic in the church, and I had seen the remarkable accuracy of a balanced battery of tests. I decided on the spot that I would show John how much I loved him, even if it killed me. And it did kill part of me — my lack of sensitivity to children. We went horseback riding together. Even though I had the manual dexterity of a palsied hippopotamus, I tried to do woodworking with him and other manual activities which he enjoyed. The real turnaround, however, came one day in a motel on the ocean front at Laguna Beach. I came into his room one morning after my enlightenment and asked, "Johnnie, wouldn't you like to go swimming with me?"

Then, as only an eleven-year-old can say it, he replied, "Nah . . . I'd rather watch television."

Before my decision to love John no matter what he said, I would have left feeling rejected; then I would have spent my time doing something I preferred doing anyway. But after the psychologist's revelation, I thought to myself, "Perhaps he is only testing me; I'll keep my sense of humor and pursue him." In a very playful manner (and this playful attitude is most important), I capered over to the TV set and turned it off. He turned it back on. I turned it off again. This happened several more times, and then we tussled around the room and over toward the door, then out the door and down the stairs, around the corner of the building, down the walkway, through the sand and into the ocean.

Then the miracle occurred. As we emerged from that first wave, he blew the water from his nose and exclaimed, "Father, I wondered how long it would take you to do this." The psychologist was right. He did want my attention. We had a wonderful weekend — more playing in the ocean, hiking along the rocky shoreline at Laguna, touring the shops of that vacation town, pleasantly dining in restaurants that *he selected*. The old pattern was broken, and we began to relate on many different levels. Incidentally, within six months John's Iowa achievement tests went up three years. He began to learn to read. But don't think that was the end of our working out a new relationship. Real love needs to be patient and persistent, enduring, kind and considerate.

John went off to college in Arizona, and he developed his own friends and his own life-style. Since my daughter lived in Phoenix (a place of rebirth for me on several occasions), the whole family gathered in Phoenix for Christmas. We were sitting in the sun at the swimming pool at our cheap motel. John was seventeen now. Without introduction he spoke to me calmly and deliberately: "Father, you know, I have never liked you very well." This was not what my bruised ego needed at that moment, but I remembered I was going to try to show love. I remembered what the headmaster of a school told parents to do when the children said that they did not like them. I replied, "John, I don't blame you; very often I don't like me either." The next year he gave me a gold tie tack of a pine cone, with a tiny diamond glistening on it. It remains one of my favorite keepsakes. He saved from his allowance to buy this gift — a symbol of how much we needed one another. Our relationship progressed to a new level.

Several years later John was living in Los Angeles. He heard that I was coming from Notre Dame to give a conference in Ojai, a hundred miles north of Los Angeles. He asked me if he could pick me up in his old Plymouth and take me to the conference. To my surprise he attended the lecture I gave the first evening. I decided to tell the story of the miracle at the beach at Laguna, but neither of us said anything about it that night as we drove to a lovely home on the ocean provided for us not far from the conference.

The next morning we got up early. We were breakfasting on bacon and eggs in a simple cafe. John initiated our conversation: "Father, did I actually say that at Laguna Beach?" I nodded assent. Then he went on: "Father, I know when I made up my mind that I would never ask you for anything again in my life." I asked him to tell me about it.

"I was seven years old. You had been reading A. Conan Doyle's *Tales of Sherlock Holmes* to my brother and me." He could even remember the author and the book! "My brother was away for several days, but I wanted you to read aloud to me anyway, and so I brought you the book and asked you to read. You said that you were too busy. I brought the book the next night, and you said that you were too busy. The same thing happened on the third night, and quite consciously I made up my mind that I would never ask *you* for anything else again in my life."

I had not realized how sensitive and needing of my love and attention this son of mine had been and was. My refusal to read had struck at him as effectively as if I had wielded a club. I even remembered the incident. Nevertheless, patient love can even make the desert burst into bloom. A deep and real relationship began to develop between us. In one family crisis with serious potential, John stuck by me and ministered to me with as much love, sensitivity and concern as I have felt from the finest of psychotherapists.

In January of 1981, Barbara and I went on a freighter trip to Southeast Asia. This seemed to us the very best place to rest and write and catch up on reading. The trip came to a disastrous end when Barbara was run over on the docks of Yokohama by a container straddler. She spent a week in the hospital until her condition stabilized, and then we flew her home to a hospital in Los Angeles. We knew that it would be at least two months before she could be released, and we did not know if she would fully recover or not. I wanted to be close enough to the hospital so that I could go in daily to spend time with her and have eucharist with her and the laying-on-of-hands for healing.

John was living not far from the hospital in a one-bedroom apartment. He invited me to live with him. He worked nights, and I was working during the day, and so we kept the bed warm most of the time. I was there in the morning when he came home from working nights at the Hyatt Regency. (He stopped to see Barbara on the way home.) I was there when he awoke in the afternoon, and we talked about all sorts of things and often went out to dinner together. I did most of the shopping, did the washing and kept the place clean and neat. These were new activities for me. And we became good friends.

While John was sleeping during the day, I attended to my mail and kept in touch with my friends. I had no specific writing project. I had long periods of time for meditation. John and I were enjoying each other.

During this time in Los Angeles, I missed the cabin that Barbara and I have in the redwoods. These trees were often in my mind and the thought came to me that we human beings have an even greater potential for growth than the redwoods; these trees start with a tiny seed and grow into the largest living things. I began to write down the thoughts that came to me, and each day a few more words sprang up in my mind. I would share these writings with Barbara when I went to see her in the evenings. (These reflections were published a few years ago as a little book, *Prayer and the Redwood Seed*.) I saw the same kind of growth occurring in all of us during this time together.

John and I got to know each other well. I tried to have his favorite foods in the kitchen, and he led me to the best restaurants. John introduced me to greater Los Angeles. On weekends we would go jogging together. He shared his favorite museums with me. I had not realized his fine artistic knowledge and taste. He took me to a museum where I saw my first Van Gogh, which captured my eyes and drew me to it from another gallery of the museum. John also shared his favorite books. We talked about everything; we could share on every level, except for one thing — a block that was later washed away.

My wife was finally released from the hospital after a two-month stay; she and I then went to stay at a friend's house to continue her convalescence. When I moved out of his apartment, John handed me a card. I opened it. On the front of it were two iguanas facing each other; one of them was weeping iguana tears. On the inside of the card were printed these words: "Iguana miss you." And then he wrote, "It seems strange how we were forced together. You have become truly my best friend. I love you more than I ever imagined. I can truly see why all of those kids have always looked up to you. I only hope that we can continue to spend time together. I hope all goes well with Mother's recovery, and if you need my help, you know that I am here."

After two months in the hospital and another two months in the home of a very gracious friend (hospitality is one of the qualities of *agape*), Barbara recovered nearly completely. We saw a lot of John and of our other son and his wife, who lived on the other side of Los Angeles. John came to realize that he had not followed his natural interest; he had always loved to cook. So he attended chef school and became a successful caterer. Barbara helped him with several of his enormous parties. We also wanted to stay in closer touch, and so Barbara and I planned that each of us would spend one week per year on vacation, traveling with him alone. We had wonderful trips together. Barbara and I lectured all over the world, so we had lots of free flight coupons, and John could provide free rooms through his work at the Hyatt. It was Indian summer.

Through no fault of his, John's business failed. He became very discouraged. He knew that he needed some help, but he knew that his close relationship with me made it impossible for me to be his therapist. On one of our trips together John had met one of my closest friends, Andy Canale, a psychologist in the Boston area. John was drawn to him both as a human being and a therapist. He wanted to work with him. But this posed a huge problem: Could John be entirely open to Andy without breaking the relationship Andy and I built over the years? Andy and I talked, and I told him that if he could be of help to John, I was willing to sacrifice even our long-standing friendship.

John and I were vacationing among the largest of the redwoods. We stopped at a pay phone so John and Andy could have their weekly talk. Afterwards we were silent for many miles as we drove on together. Then John began to pour out his very deepest pains and hurts, which he had never been able to share with me before. Quite naturally a large part of his pain was my absence as a father when he was a child. He had just described this hurt to Andy, who had said, "Why don't you tell your father about all this?" He knew that I would want to know, and that I needed to know. As we drove through the giant redwoods, the hurt of the fatherless, abandoned child in John flooded out of him. Talking about this pain was such a relief that he broke down and could no longer drive. I drove on as he continued to let his hurts drain from him until most of his psychic infection had emptied out. He became quiet. We walked among the redwoods in my favorite grove of majestic trees, many of them two thousand years old. A peace and serenity enveloped both of us. We finished the day with a superb meal. It was like Babette's Feast. We both slept peacefully. The final barriers had fallen down.

Love Is Forever

John could share nearly everything now. He discovered that the world of Los Angeles and Beverly Hills was poisoning him. He needed a simpler life, closer to the earth. He spent a month on the big island of Hawaii. His enthusiasm and vigor returned. He placed his car and all his belongings in a seagoing container and moved to Kona. He made new friends immediately. We visited him there for a week after he was established in a house with friends; John took us to all of his favorite places on that magnificent and dynamic island — to volcanoes, fields of orchids, waterfalls, forests and deserts, and a hundred different seascapes. He had a four-wheel-drive car, and he could take us anywhere. John shared what he had learned about the original Hawaiian culture, which fascinated all three of us.

Some time later the phone rang. It was John; he had come down with an incurable form of encephalitis. He was beginning to be paralyzed and had blackouts, each of which could have been the end. He was able to ask now for what he wanted; he knew that we knew all about him and loved him even more. "Would you please come and take over?" he asked. When I answered that I could come in two days, he replied: "Tomorrow would be better." The next day he met me at the airport in a wheelchair and apologized that he could not carry my bags. In a week I made arrangements to care for him until we returned. I had to conduct a week's conference, to which both Barbara and I were committed.

Ten days later Barbara and I returned to Kona to stay with him as long as he lived. As we made plans together, he had only four requests of us. He wished to die by the sea, in his own bed; he wanted to be kept as comfortable as possible; and he wanted no heroic means used to keep him alive. Later we learned another desire on his part: He wanted to handle his own sickness with an excellent doctor who understood him. Nearly every week some of his friends from the mainland came to visit him; his new friends on the island were incredibly helpful and present to him.

He and Andy Canale continued their weekly talks. Not long

before he died, John told Andy of a dream: He dreamed he was out purchasing camping equipment for an adventurous trip that he would be making soon, and he had all the money he could use. John had no fear of death or of the mysterious journey he was about to make. He was, however, getting ready for the journey. When I talked with Andy about describing how much I learned from John in those last days, he reminded me of John's dream. John was at peace: He was getting together what he needed for that adventure. His condition is well described by Stanislav Grof in his book, *Beyond the Brain: Birth, Death and Transcendence in Psychotherapy*. The dying who have experienced a glimpse of what I call eternal life "now see their current life problems and past biographical material from a completely new perspective. From this new perspective, the events of their present existence do not seem to have the same overwhelming relevance that they had before. In addition, the goal of the psychological work is now clear; further self-exploration resembles the broadening and clearing of a road to a known destination, rather than blind digging in a dark tunnel."[1]

John lived the last months of life as fully as he lived the rest of his life. We were able to go out for dinner nearly every night until the last ten days, when he was bedridden. With the help of a friend — a male trained nurse — he even made a trip to a convention he wanted to attend on another island, and he went sailing in a catamaran only three weeks before he died.

During the nights Barbara stayed with John. During the days I was with him. One day as I was sitting beside him, I again asked his forgiveness for not having known how to be the caring father that he had needed as a child. He replied, "What you are doing now makes up and more for anything that you didn't do at any other time." Another time he said, "Father, what would you be doing if you were not here with me?" I said that I had been asked to write a book and was halfway through it. He replied in an authoritative tone: "I sleep a good portion of the afternoon. Get out my Canon Star Five typewriter and finish the book." So I got out the typewriter and finished the first draft while I was still sitting with him. *Reaching: The Journey to Fulfillment* became a very different book than I had anticipated. It started as a quiet meditation on living the full life; as I sat beside my dying son, however, the book became a passionate vision of crippling illness and life beyond death.

At times the pain of seeing his body disintegrating before my eyes was almost more than I could take. On one occasion, close friends of ours visited us; John had lived with them while Barbara and I were at Notre Dame. I looked forward to seeing them. As I was taking my friend for a ride, he told me that he was dying of cancer. I was glad he could share this with me; it showed me that I was not fighting this battle alone. We both faced a deadly enemy. But it seemed hopeless. I needed some time to be quiet and pray; I was overwhelmed by too much death. I got away by myself that afternoon. Using the method that I described in the first chapter, I spoke directly to the dark presence that was dragging me and John and my friend and everyone else with heavy chains into the darkness. The following words flowed out:

Death, you strike again. You laugh at me and speak:

You were frightened when I touched your own blood
And made you the oldest one of all,
The last one to survive. Now you watch
As I crush your son before your eyes.
Remember how they slew his sons as the captured king
Stood by and then they blinded him as well.
That bloody scene was my fine work.
And your good friend eaten away from within,
Like so many that you have known. And now you —
You and all you love, all in my hand
Crushed to sand like rocks against
Relentless waves. So ends all love.

We stand glaring at each other. He spits into my face. I wipe away the slime, I do not budge. And then I cry out:

You can strike me down, Death,
But I will not submit to your monstrosity.
Heap corpse upon corpse, and still you will not win.
You cannot kill the spirit, mind, or soul.
That is why you stoop to horror.
You are so afraid. You have lost your power.
I remember now. Strange how I forgot.
Death and evil — close kin you are and both
Have been defeated, routed, spoiled.
I need not fear you. I can go on.

The heavy darkness rises, and I can see the mountaintops again.
Courage and hope return, and I begin a long and busy day with a
new attitude and some joy.

This restoration came in less than an hour. These words and
several of the following pages are taken from *Reaching: Journey to
Fulfillment,* written in the white heat of facing death and what lies
beyond it. I cannot nor do I wish to relive the state in which I
wrote these words, and so I will quote some of them here and
later more.[2] They are the best I can do to describe the final goal
of the art of Christian love.

I lived with death for four months. Up until about twenty-five
years ago death was even more unmentionable than sex in polite
society. Yet all of us die and many people who have been raised
in our materialistic Western civilization take it as one of the
givens that human beings cease to exist with the demise of the
body, the disintegration of the physical organism. And it is this
view, I think, that has made death so unspeakable: Total extinc-
tion of our loved ones or of ourselves is hard to face. If this life is
all we have, then as long as it gives us some pleasure, we would
prefer not to be annihilated. We can get sick and be healed and
then live on until we get sick again, but at the end of the line, all
of us die. The best and wisest and the worst and vilest all go down
to the same democratic realm of the grave and death; for all of us,
the time comes to die.

Love demands that we do all we can for the sick, the disabled and the broken. However, if there is nothing to hope for beyond this vale of tears, then many of us who think about the implications of this lack of hope will look with utter despair upon our total existence. I am convinced, then, that true health and healing in this world demands that there be something better in store for us. True and final healing occurs only on the other side of despair, suffering and death. *True healing requires residence in the kingdom of heaven, the fellowship of love.*

No one has stated this conviction better than Pinchas Lapide, a Jewish scholar who lived through the Holocaust. Lapide writes that life makes no sense without the transformation of life beyond death, and he describes the resurrection of Jesus as a momentous historical example of the power of God over death. These are Lapide's words:

> All honest theology is a theology of catastrophe, a theology that receives its impulse from the misery and the nobility of our human nature.
> • from the fear of death, from the will to live, and from the great hope that not everything is an end when death comes;
> • a hope that arises from an anticipation of that incomprehensible infinity and final reality which we call God;
> • a hope that cannot acquiesce in the thought that our existence begins with birth pangs and a whimper — only to end with a final rattle of agony;
> • a hope that tears, death and mourning will not have the last word;
> • a hope that draws from its confidence "upward" the courage to look "ahead"; courage beyond dying to a life beyond the grave which deprives death of its sting in order to give our life a meaning which cannot perish or decay.
> That is the quintessence of the biblical faith in the resurrection, both of Jews and Christians.

Lapide concludes that the founding of the Jewish state gave hope to modern Jews, much as the resurrection of Jesus empowered the early Christians.[3]

What is the fulfillment of heaven? It is that eternal state of being where we will be comforted, made heirs of all earth's real treasure and have our deepest longings filled and transformed into greater longings. We shall receive pardon and mercy and love and then know the joy of being part of the family of Love, working and playing divine games. Boethius wrote: "Heaven is the simultaneous fruition of life without bounds." It is like a bud bursting into eternal bloom, like a bloom ripening into eternal fruit, like a train emerging from a dark tunnel into the full light of day and then going on to a superb alpine valley.

We can tell much about a house by the furniture in it. We can tell much about a public place by the people who frequent it. We can learn much about a country by the people from it. And we can tell much about heaven by the people whom we know are there. Heaven is the reality in which we find the kind, humble, fine, noble, courageous, understanding, forgiving, striving, childlike, loving spirits we have loved on earth. This is their home, in which they find fulfillment and consummation.

Farewell

Death is birth into a new dimension of reality. For those who wish the transformation and fulfillment of heaven, death is an entrance into greater joy than we can imagine. But dying is another matter; it can be painful, grim and heart-rending for the dying and for those who watch with them.

As I wrote these words, my wife and I had been watching for four months the slow physical and finally mental disintegration of a handsome and sensitive young man, our son. Paul Tournier's book *Creative Suffering* was a most helpful aid to survival during this period.[4] Tournier writes that the conscious descent toward death is the supreme deprivation from an earthy point of view;

the dying, therefore, need fellowship and companionship and love more than any other people.

Loneliness, aloneness, is one of the most difficult burdens that human beings can bear, and we die alone — we take the final journey all by ourselves. The importance of being with the dying can hardly be exaggerated. It prepares them for the last stage of their earthly journey. And for those who minister to them, it can be a time of self-giving that is infinitely rewarding. These four months with John brought us closer to each other than the three of us had ever been. It was a painful privilege, a great release and a great loss, a grief-filled victory that leaves a deep emptiness and yet a sense of fulfillment in the two of us who are left.

One of the tasks of the shaman in many religions is to accompany the dying to the other side. Indeed, one important aspect of any religious calling has been ministering to the dying, listening to them, being willing to talk about their doubts and fears, being with them. Everything I have written about love applies particularly to our treatment of the dying: They especially need to be loved. Elisabeth Kübler-Ross awakened the medical and religious community to the fact that many of us are afraid of the dying, and we tend to shun them.

If we have not dealt with our own fear of death, we will find it difficult, if not impossible, to minister with love to the dying. If we basically believe that death is the end and that there is nothing beyond, it will be virtually impossible for us to sustain the dying with hope. Our unconscious attitude will seep through any of our efforts at being upbeat. True caring, sensitivity to their needs, never forcing our belief systems upon them and faithfulness are essential for ministering to the dying. And we must not minimize the pain that death inflicts: Even though the Church's picture of the communion of saints conveys a real truth, we on this side of death do lose the touch and intimate physical caring that our beloved gave us when he or she was alive. And we lose the closeness that touch and smile and words gave to our beloved and to us. Death is a great divide, one through which the dying pass alone and one that causes us deep sorrow. Is there any greater pain than losing a partner with whom we have lived for fifty years, or a child whom we have nurtured, cared for, let go and then received back as a close friend?

And yet we must let our beloved go. I received a letter from a woman whose son had been killed under tragic circumstances. The woman had experienced an early-morning vision in which her dead son returned to her to let her know that he was all right and that her holding on to him was stifling him. So we need to strike a balance between hanging on too tightly to the dead whom we have loved and forgetting them, having them slip from our hearts altogether.

While I was sitting by our son's bed, the following words came to me while John was sleeping. I call them, "My Son at the Door of Death."

> Fear not for me. I'm not afraid.
> A new adventure awaits me,
> A new more brilliant being
> Is about to birth
> Into a different space and time.
> The garden of heaven and those abiding there
> Are calling me insistently. They want me soon.
> They sing of my courage and frustration,
> Of years of seeking, relentless searching. . . .
> So many roads that petered out
> In scorching desert and burning sand
> And still I kept on, was guided.
> These voices promise
> To answer all my questions
> With love unbounded, limitless.
> They offer intimacy, closeness, far richer
> Than I had dared to hope for, and wisdom, too,
> And living water drawn from the deepest well
> That holds the secret mysteries safe
> From vain and curious wanderers.
> The voices also sing of love and loving,

Of giving all I had and only at this moment
Knowing that my arrow struck its mark.

Do not hold me back. I'll be with you still
In fuller measure than I've ever given.
The sun is rising from the sea
As one by one the stars are lost in light.
The broken has been mended.
I can be loved and love.
It is time to go.
Pushed beyond the limits
Of death and pain and hope,
I find the real
Eternal Love.

A day or two later I read these words to John. Still later he asked
me for a copy of them. He shared them with a friend, and she
later told Barbara and me that John had said to her, "Father
understands how I feel." The friend gave us a great gift when she
shared his statement with us.

When John died, we had eucharist and the burial office at his
bedside with the roaring of the waves as accompaniment to our
words. When I watched his body leave his home by the sea, the
words that Horatio spoke at Hamlet's death rose from the well
of memory:

Now cracks a noble heart. Good-night, sweet prince,
And flights of angels sing thee to thy rest.

I spoke them to our other son, who stood beside me. John was
entering a new adventure. How much his faith sustained us.

Alan Paton was one of the most magnificent human beings
Barbara and I ever met. He combined deep religious conviction
with a passion for justice and political action; he lived the message of his book *Cry, the Beloved Country*. His wife was his editor,
and she stood with him in his political struggles in South Africa.
When she died, he was devastated. He wrote out his remem-

brances of her as if he were talking to her. When he finished, his paralyzing grief and depression had lifted. He published this writing as a tribute to her in the book, *For You, Departed*. Barbara and I read this book as we drove to the airport to be with John in his final illness.

In the years that have passed since our son's death, we have found that writing down our memories of our life together with John has given us a sense of John's presence. Writing about love has also brought to a new completion the fellowship and intimacy that we experienced in four months of daily interaction and personal care-taking. The finality and mystery of death remain, but this sharing of memories and love has not fallen unnoticed into the void. This sharing of how much John taught us seems to be received and acknowledged by one who is now on the other side of the communion of saints.

I conclude these reflections on the greatest gift with a prayer that Barbara and I prayed for John's fulfillment and for our own. These words are a response to the feelings that we articulated for John and that he endorsed as his very own; they are adapted from a prayer that a friend sent to Alan Paton at his wife's death, which helped him greatly. In his book Paton quoted this prayer, and the words opened our hearts to a new way of praying for our beloved departed. This is still our prayer for our beloved John:

> O Mother-Father God, ever loving and ever living, the final reality in which all souls find their completion, rest and fulfillment, we pray for him whom you know and love far more deeply than we can even imagine. Give him your light and love, for which he sought so fervently. In your mercy heal, strengthen, enlighten and guide him as he steps further into the unbounded and mysterious vistas of eternity. May his immortal being reveal more and more the infinite potential of wisdom, joy and love with which you endow the human soul. May he know the intimate fellowship of the children of God and become an ambassador of your caring and peace to all dimensions of your universe.

O Gracious One, let him know how much we love and miss his physical presence and long to be with him. Grant that he may be allowed to guide and guard our journey until we meet in that condition where partings cease. Until then give us a sense of his loving presence. Heal all his wounds inflicted by an insensitive and unconscious society. Let us minister in any way we can to his growth, peace and joy. Let us do nothing that keeps us from fellowship together in the communion of saints. We ask this of you, a loving God who created us, saw our misery, came among us, suffered with us, suffered for us and by rising again opened to us the portals of eternal life. Amen.

Notes

The Journey Home

1. This letter was written by Robert Johnson, the well-known author who has published many books beginning with *He, She and We.*

2. My book, *Can Christians Be Educated?* (Birmingham, Alabama: Religious Education Press, 1977) is an attempt to show how people can be educated religiously today within the materialistic atheism of our time.

3. I discuss the relationship of emotions, religion and health in chapter 11 of *Healing and Christianity* (Minneapolis: Augsburg Fortress, 1995).

4. Morton Kelsey, *The Other Side of Silence, A Guide to Christian Meditation* (Mahwah, New Jersey: Paulist Press, 1976), p. 304. Slightly altered to fit this context.

5. These thoughts on the art of Christian love were first expressed in years of sermons following my experience in the plane. They were first published as *The Art of Christian Love* (Pecos, New Mexico: Dove Publications, 1974). When that pamphlet went out of print, I wrote a book combining psychological insights with the religious ones (*Caring, How Can We Love One Another?* [Mahwah, New Jersey: Paulist Press, 1981]). For fifteen years I have been lecturing on this subject all over the world. In each conference I have been given new material. Life has also given me a great number of new insights. This book is an amplification of the original pamphlet into a full book. Those who are interested in the psychological implications are referred to *Caring, How Can We Love One Another?*

The Gospel within the Gospel

1. Matthew 20 describes the situation in Palestine at that time. Few owned their own land.

2. Recent archaeology has demonstrated the social chaos of the time in which Jesus was ministering in Galilee and Judea. Elaborate palaces of the priestly families have been uncovered. Recent excavations indi-

cate Roman control and reveal that Roman cities were the centers of power. Herod Antipas built Tiberias on the site of an ancient cemetery, and so it was unclean in Jewish ritual law. His Jewish subjects would not come near it. Herod Antipas had to import Gentiles to fill his magnificent new city. No wonder Jesus, who was seeking the lost sheep of Israel, avoided it and that it is also never mentioned in the New Testament. Sepphoris, another Graeco-Roman city flourishing a few miles from Nazareth is also never mentioned in the New Testament. An excellent picture of the chaotic social scene is described by Neil Asher Silberman, "Searching for Jesus: The Politics of First Century Judea," *Archaeology*, November/December 1994, pp. 30-41.

3. I use my own translation of this passage, Luke 15:2, to give the full flavor of the Greek. These four parables are in Luke 15:4-16:9.

4. Laurens Van der Post, *The Face Beside the Fire* (New York: William Morrow and Company, Inc., 1953), p. 268.

5. Two books by Kenneth E. Bailey explain many aspects of Jesus' stories from the standpoint of Semitic life: *The Cross and the Prodigal* (St. Louis: Concordia Publishing House, 1973), and *Through Peasant Eyes* (Grand Rapids, Michigan: W. B. Eerdmans Publishing House, 1950). In my book *Resurrection: Release from Oppression* (Mahway, New Jersey: Paulist Press, 1973), I use much of this material to explain the essence of Jesus' teaching.

6. Walter Wink, *Transforming Bible Study* (Nashville: Abington, 1980). See particularly Appendix 2, pp. 159-62. My book *God, Dreams and Revelation* (Minneapolis: Augsburg Fortress, 1991) explains how the dream and its symbols were considered revelatory in the Western Church until the enlightenment and have never ceased being understood in this way in the Orthodox tradition.

The Greatest Gift in the World

1. Readers can verify these facts if they consult Robert Young, *Analytical Concordance to the Bible* (Grand Rapids, Michigan: Eerdmans Publishing Company, 1972), pp. 622-24, and *Webster's New Twentieth Century Dictionary* (New York: The World Publishing Company, 1971), pp. 1071-72.

2. J. Bruce Long provides an excellent survey of the great emphasis on love in all the major world religions, *The Encyclopedia of Religions*, ed. Mircea Eliade (New York: Macmillan, 1987), vol. 9, pp. 31-40.

3. James Baldwin, quoted in Richard Coan in *Hero, Artists, Sage or Saint* (New York: Columbia University Press, 1977), p. 301.

4. Aldous Huxley, *Tomorrow and Tomorrow and Tomorrow, and Other Essays* (New York: Harper & Brothers, 1956), p. 68.

5. Larry Dossey, M.D., *Healing Words: The Power of Prayer and the Practice of Medicine* (San Francisco: Harper, 1993), p. 117. Also see my book, *Healing and Christianity* (Minneapolis: Augsburg Fortress, 1995).

6. The evidence for the fallible nature of mathematics is found in Ernest Nagel and James R. Newman, *Gödel's Proof* (New York: New York University Press, 1958); in *The Anthropic Cosmological Principle* (Oxford: Oxford University Press, 1989), John D. Barrow, a mathematical astronomer, and Frank J. Tipler, a mathematical physicist, present overwhelming evidence in great detail that the universe did not develop just by chance. The earth seems to have been created specifically to provide for the emergence of life. The universe was created so that it and its Creator could be observed.

John Polkinghorne (formerly a professor of small-particle mathematics in the nucleus of the atom at Cambridge University and now an Anglican clergyperson and president of Queen's College, Cambridge) has drawn the theological implications of the mystery of creation revealed in modern physics in three remarkable books: *One Word* (London: SPCK, 1986), *Science and Providence* (Boston: Shambahala, 1989). Polkinghorne's most recent books are: *Reason and Reality* (Philadelphia: Trinity Publishing International, 1992), which contains the finest description of quantum mechanics that I have discovered, and also his 1993-94 Gifford Lectures, *Science and Christian Belief: Theological Reflections of a Bottom-up Thinker* (London: SPCK, 1994). A popular presentation of the mystery of matter and the failure of mechanical and material explanations to account for the freedom that exists on the quantum level is contained in Paul Davies and John Gribbin, *The Matter Myth* (New York: Simon & Schuster, 1992).

James Trefil surveys the new biological evidence for the statement of the biologist, Cyril Ponnamperuma, "The business of the Universe is creating life" in an article "However it began on Earth, life may have been inevitable," *Smithsonian*, Vol. 25, Number 11, Feb. 1995.

One of the leading living physicists, Roger Penrose, has produced a fine study of the human mind showing the impossibility of creating a computer mind that can truly understand and think, *Shadows of the Mind, A Search for the Missing Science of Consciousness* (New York: Oxford University Press, 1994).

7. *Complete Poems of Emily Dickinson*, ed. Thomas H. Johnson (Boston: Little Brown and Co., 1960), p. 432.

8. Nouwen's experience is described in *Weavings, A Journal of Christian Life*, Volume 4, Number 6, November/December, 1989, pp. 16-17,

19, 22. An expanded account of this text has been published: Henri Nouwen, *Beyond the Mirror* (New York: Crossroad, 1990). I have used this passage often in lecturing; it touches people deeply. Nearly everyone in the hall will raise their hands when asked if they know of Nouwen's works, but a very few or none have heard of this recent and personal book. His experience is simply not taken seriously by most of the academic or administrative boards of the mainline Churches. Italics are mine.

9. Ibid., p. 17.

10. Ibid., p. 19.

11. Ibid., p. 22.

12. This letter was written by Gayle Muessle, 340 American Drive, #3, Lago Vista, Texas 78645. Used with permission.

13. Thomas Wolfe, *You Can't Go Home Again* (New York: Harper & Brothers, 1940), p. 743. The letter was quoted from an article on Thomas Wolfe in *Life*, July 1966.

14. *St. John of the Cross*, trans. E. Allison Peers (Garden City, New York: Doubleday & Company, Inc. 1959), pp. 67f.

15. This is found in my book, *Companions On the Inner Way* (New York: Crossroad, 1983), pp. 149-50.

16. Johann Wolfgang von Goethe, *Faust*, second part, Act 5, line 11935.

17. *The Comedy of Dante Alighieri: Cantica III, Paradise*, trans. Dorothy L. Sayers and Barbara Reynolds (Baltimore: Penguin Books, 1963), p. 347. Reprinted by permission of one of the translators and Penguin Books.

18. George Herbert, "Love," in *The Home Book of Verse*, ed. Burton Egbert Stevenson (New York: Henry Holt & Co., 1918), p. 3718.

The Depth and Beauty of Love

1. In my book *Prayer and the Redwood Seed* (New York: Continuum Publishing Group, 1991) I examine poetry that pictures the importance of light for every living thing. Quiet human openness to the divine light is as important to our spiritual growth as light is important to the redwood tree.

2. These are a few of the most important statements about love found in 1 Peter 4:8, 1 John 4:16, 20. If we do not realize the importance of love, we often do not see how often it is mentioned. This truth was demonstrated at the Cognitive Learning Laboratory at Harvard University. An

ordinary set of playing cards was altered by painting the black six of spades red. The card was inserted in a deck and cards were shown to a large number of subjects in this experiment. Practically no one described the odd card correctly; they called it either an ordinary black six of spades or the six of diamonds. In the same way we can fail to see the importance of love in the New Testament. Unless we are taught to see clearly, we simply will not see how important love is to the teaching of Jesus. A practical exercise is to read through the New Testament and mark every reference to love.

3. For many years I have been interested in the gifts of the spirit (sometimes referred to as charisms) largely because they had been ignored by most modern theologians. I have published the following: *Tongue Speaking* (New York: Crossroad, 1981), *Healing and Christianity* (Minneapolis: Augsburg, 1995), *God, Dreams and Revelation* (Minneapolis: Augsburg, 1991), *Discernment* (Mahwah, New Jersey: Paulist Press, 1978), *The Christian and the Supernatural* (Minneapolis: Augsburg, 1976); *The Other Side of Silence* (Mahwah, New Jersey: Paulist Press, 1976); on the theology of gifts, *Encounter with God* (Mahwah, New Jersey: Paulist Press, 1987).

The passage that introduces Paul's Hymn to Love has been mistranslated in most English editions of the New Testament. My paraphrase of 1 Corinthians 12:31b above is based on a paper by Dr. Francis Whiting and my own study. Paul is not saying that love is better than the gifts; he is saying that love is the best and only pathway. Even the powerful gifts of the spirit as well as all other human gifts must be undergirded with love. Francis Whiting in an unpublished paper, "On the Translation of 1 Corinthians 12:31," makes this very clear. He writes: "Let us look at the Greek words with the English translation beneath:

"Verse 12a:

zeloute	*de*	*ta*	*charismata*	*ta*	*meizona*
desire	but	the	charism	the	greater

kai	*eti*	*kath*	*huperbolen*	*odon*	*humin*	*deiknumi*
and	further	very	the best	way	for you	I'll point out

"Now let's put that in good idiomatic English: 'Now desire the greater gifts and, further, I'll point out for you the very best way [to gain and use a spiritual gift]'" (pp. 2-3).

Whiting then points out that there has been little interest in experiential religion or the gifts of the spirit in the Western Christian Church and so the translators had little accepted experience to guide them in their translation. He then goes on:

"There is no comparison in 1 Corinthians 12:31. Look at the following evidences. First of all *The Expositor's Greek Testament* (Grand Rapids:

Eerdmans, n.d.) the section 'St. Paul's First Epistle to the Corinthians' by G. G. Findley, professor of Biblical literature, Headingley College England: He allows, '*Love* is the path to power in the Church; all loveless abilities, endowments, sacrifices are, from the Christian point of view, simply *good for nothing*.' Then he goes on: 'kath uperbolen' is superlative, not comparative. Paul is not pointing out 'a *more* excellent way' than that of seeking and using the charisms of chapter 12 . . . but a 'super-excellent way' . . . to win them.

"And now listen to the famed A. T. Robertson: 'In order to gain the greater gifts, I show you a way *par excellence* beyond all comparison (superlative in this adjunct, not comparative). I show you a supremely excellent way' " (*Word Pictures in the New Testament*, Archibald Thomas Robertson, Nashville: Sunday School Board of the Southern Baptist Church, 1931).

As I have noted before, there are fourteen different Greek words that are translated love. However, the most common Greek word for love, *eros*, is not found in the New Testament. That word is used in Plato to denote physical, sexual love, but also a pure love of soul for soul. This kind of love for another's soul could lead to love of the one who created the soul — the creating Divine. Plato considered *eros* one of the divine gifts along with prophecy, healing and artistic inspiration. *Eros* was also the name for a Greek god who was sometimes perceived as the ultimate creating divinity. *Agape* is the most common word used to describe love in the New Testament; it is the word used in this magnificent, poetic description of love in 1 Corinthians 13. The Greek verb *agapao* was used in Greek literature from the time of Homer on. It could refer to the love of one human being for another, love of supernatural beings for one another and for human beings and human love for the gods. It also was used to describe striving for material things or anything that was desired as in "I love candy." The noun *agape* came into use only in the first century before Christ. It was necessary for Paul to tell his Greek followers the precise meaning of Christian love, what this word meant to the leaders of the Christian community. The verb and the noun, *agapeo* and *agape*, both convey the sense of a gift of the divine and of the human striving that could be directed toward the divine or toward human beings or to the selfish desire for whatever one wished. It was translated by the Latin word *caritas*, which conveys the same meanings that we are describing. In his widely read book, *Agape and Eros* (Philadelphia: The Westminister Press, 1953), Anders Nygren states that there is no desire in Christian love. It is by faith alone that we are given Christian love. He gives to the word *agape* a meaning that it does not have in Greek. He does not believe that Augustine's statement was true: God made us restless that we might find our rest in him. In Nygren's study we have no part in receiving the gift of love. We cannot by our effort do anything to increase our love. This is not the meaning of the Greek word, *agape*.

4. In the ancient texts we find different Greek words, but the meaning is quite clear. If we are boasting as we give our bodies to be burned as a sacrifice, we gain nothing.

5. Francis Whiting, "On the Translation of 1 Corinthians 12:31," p. 3.

6. This is my own paraphrase of the Greek Romans 12:6-8.

7. I am grateful to the unknown woman who handed me the hand-written sheet many years ago. This paper encouraged me to study the Greek of this incomparable ode to love and to add to her list.

8. This English word is taken directly from the Greek; it is simply transliterated and has the same meaning as the Greek. The Greek letters are replaced by their English equivalents.

9. As I have studied the Greek text, I have come to a new appreciation of Paul's knowledge of Greek and his literary genius. In four and a half short verses Paul uses twenty different Greek words to describe love. In addition, each of these words conveys a bewildering number of different meanings. For example, *stegei* (forbearing above) means: to pass over in silence, to keep confidential, to cover, and also to bear, to stand, to endure. The word is related to the common word for roof. Most translators pick and use only one meaning and miss the point that all six meanings are characteristic of love. Five different translations in my library pick only one of the six. I doubt if it is possible to translate word for word from an incredibly complex language, Greek, into another language equally complex, English. Could not Paul have used this word just because its many meanings applied to love? If one is to render Paul's full meaning, it is necessary to use paraphrases, as J. B. Phillips does to a certain extent in *The New Testament in Modern English*. Learning the original language of a text is almost necessary to understand it. I use only three English words in the list of love's characteristics that are not specifically drawn from Paul's description. However, attentive, consoling and playful are implied in the other words.

It is my feeling that 1 Corinthians 13 was not just written at the time of writing to the Corinthians but was carefully worked out and used as a homily or blessing at eucharist by Paul.

10. A careful study of the relative commonness of these experiences is to be found in G. Scott Sparrow, *I Am with You Always, True Stories of Encounters with Jesus* (New York: Bantam, 1995). I provided an introduction for this book.

11. Fyodor Dostoyevsky, *The Brothers Karamazov*, trans. Andrew R. MacAndrew (New York: Bantam, 1970), vol. 2, pp. 66-67.

12. Quoted from an article by Martin Copenhaver, Burlington Free Press, September 1990. The Greek word *chresteuomai*, to be kind, is found only in Christian literature. The virtue of kindness was not very popular in either Greek or Roman society. The word is derived from the ancient Greek word, *chrestos*, meaning useful, suitable, worthy, good. Morally the Greek word came to mean goodness, kindness, generosity. In that sense it is found twenty times throughout the New Testament. The idea of the verb is that love is kind, loving, merciful, generous, benevolent. In speaking of the fifth beatitude — often translated, "Blessed are the merciful; they shall receive mercy" — Clement of Alexander uses this verb *to be kind*: "Blessed are the kind; they shall receive kindness."

The Greek word *christos*, meaning the anointed one or the Messiah, was also a personal name commonly used at the time of Paul. The word *chrestos*, meaning kindly and good, was pronounced like *christos*. The pagan world probably understood the words "Jesus Christ" simply as the full name of the Christians' deity. It is an interesting synchronicity that Christ in Greek is so close to the word kind.

13. See the previous chapter, "The Greatest Gift in the World," note 6.

14. *Letters of St. Catherine of Siena*, ed. by Via Scudder (Boston: Little Brown, 1934).

15. I have written four books that deal directly with life after death: *Afterlife* (New York: Crossroad, 1982); *Resurrection, Release from Oppression* (Mahwah, New Jersey: Paulist Press, 1985); *Through Defeat to Victory* (New York: Continuum Publishing Group, 1994). *Reaching: the Journey to Fulfillment* (Minneapolis: Augsburg Fortress, 1994) was written at the bedside of my dying son as I was wrestling with the evil of suffering and death that confronted me.

16. In two books I deal extensively with the subject of human development, using a model developed by C. G. Jung: Morton Kelsey, *Companions on the Inner Way: The Art of Spiritual Direction* (New York: Crossroad, 1987), pp. 177-95; *Reaching: The Journey to Fulfillment* (Minneapolis: Augsburg Fortress, 1994), pp. 53-55. The best full study of human development within the religious context is: Elizabeth Liebert, *Changing Life Patterns: Adult Development in Spiritual Direction* (Mahwah, New Jersey: Paulist Press, 1992). Her work is based on a model developed in Jane Loevinger's book, *Ego Development*.

17. I deal with the subject in greater depth in *Reaching: The Journey to Fulfillment*, chapter 9.

18. This is my paraphrase of 1 Corinthians 13:6. Paul uses two different words to express mild satisfaction and unbounded joy. The

word *unrighteousness* has the many meanings I have used, and the word *truth* is one of the noblest words in the Greek language.

19. John Masefield, *Poems* (New York: Macmillan, 1953), pp. 51-52.

20. Robert Evans and Thomas Parker, *Christian Theology: A Case Study Approach* (New York: Harper & Row, 1976), p. 91.

Who Is My Neighbor

1. This whole story is told in Luke 9:51-56, 10:17-37.

2. Few psychologists have expressed more vividly the pain and importance of self-knowledge than C. G. Jung, *Modern Man in Search of a Soul* (New York: Harcourt Brace Jovanovich, 1955), pp. 243-46.

3. *Western Spirituality: Historical Roots, Ecumenical Routes*, ed. Matthew Fox (Notre Dame, Indiana: Fides/Clarentian, 1979), p. 252.

4. These reflections were first presented at the Annual Forum of Christian Laity of Chicago in 1991 and then published in abridged form as Leaflet #89, *Who Is My Neighbor* (Pecos, New Mexico: Dove Publications, n.d.).

5. Andrew Canale, *Beyond Depression* (Rockport, Massachusetts: Element Books, 1992).

6. In *Healing and Christianity* (Minneapolis: Augsburg Fortress, 1995) I have provided the only comprehensive study of the history of healing in Christianity. This quotation is found on page 117.

7. Elizabeth O'Connor has described this program in *Servant Leaders, Servant Structures* (Washington, D.C.: The Servant Leadership School, 1991). I have written a book on how to teach adults and children the art of Christian living, of which Christian love is an essential part: *Can Christians Be Educated?* compiled and edited by Harold William Burgress (Birmingham, Alabama: Religious Education Press, 1977).

8. Walter Wink, *Engaging the Powers, Discernment and Resistance in a World of Domination* (Minneapolis: Augsburg Fortress, 1992).

9. Laurens Van der Post, *The Face Beside the Fire* (New York: William Morrow and Company, Inc., 1953), p. 268.

10. Ibid., p. 10.

Silence, Love and Prayer

1. Printed on a small card and sent to an acquaintance by Mother Teresa.

2. 2 Corinthians 12. Paul uses the same word *hyperbole* to describe his

transforming experience on the road to Damascus, the same word he used to describe the unsurpassed importance of love in 1 Corinthians 12:31.

3. Quoted in Deepak Chopra, *The Seven Spiritual Laws of Success: A Practical Guide to Fulfillment of Your Dreams* (San Rafael, California: Amber-Allen Publishing, 1944), p. 20.

4. Thomas Carlyle, *Sartor Resortus*, book 3, chapter 3.

5. Soren Kierkegaard, *Fear and Trembling* and *The Sickness unto Death*, trans. W. Lowrie (Garden City, New York: Doubleday, n.d.), pp. 197ff. and 22.

6. To my surprise my two most popular books have been *The Other Side of Silence: A Guide to Christian Meditation* (Mahwah, New Jersey: Paulist Press, 1976), and *Dreams: A Way to Listen to God* (Mahwah, New Jersey: Paulist Press, 1978). The first is a serious study of the importance of silence in Christian prayer and of the images that emerge in silence; the second is a short, simple method of using the practice of Christian dream interpretation (which has been used by many Christians throughout the history of the Church). Another study of dreams is my book on the history of dream interpretation in the Old Testament, the New Testament and the history of the Christian Church right up to the present: *God, Dreams and Revelation: A Christian Interpretation of Dreams* (Minneapolis, Minnesota: Augsburg, 1991).

7. A careful statistical study of the number of people having such experiences is found in Andrew Greeley, *The Sociology of the Paranormal: A Reconnaissance* (Beverly Hills, California: Sage Publications, 1975).

8. Keeping a written record of their religious lives is one way many profound Christians have shared the mystery of divine Love with others on the religious journey. I have written a guide to Christian journal keeping, *Adventure Inward: Christian Growth Through Personal Journal Writing* (Minneapolis, Minnesota: Augsburg, 1980).

9. Aldous Huxley, *The Doors of Perception* (New York: Harper and Row, 1970), pp. 22f.

10. I have discussed in depth the history of Christian dream interpretation in *God, Dreams and Revelation* (Minneapolis, Minnesota: Augsburg, 1991). *Dreams, Visions & Prophecies of Don Bosco* (New Rochelle, New York: Don Bosco Publications, 1986) provides a full account of his experiences.

11. The above encounter with silence is taken from *Adventure Inward* (Minneapolis, Minnesota: Augsburg, 1980), pp. 53-55. The entire last chapter of *The Other Side of Silence*, "Windows Inward," is made up of

reflections from my journals. My book *Prayer and the Redwood Seed* (New York: Continuum, 1991), was written as my wife recovered from a devastating accident. *Reaching: The Journal to Fulfillment* (San Francisco: Harper Collins, 1990) was written at the bedside of our dying son. Nearly every book I have written contains excerpts from the journals I have kept for fifty years.

12. *My Life and Love Are One*, by Susan Polis Schwartz and Nancy Y. Hoffman (Boulder, Colorado: Continental Publishing, Blue Mountain Arts, 1976), pp. 14-15. Selections from *Dear Theo: The Autobiography of Vincent van Gogh*, ed. by Irving and Jean Stone (New York: Doubleday, 1937).

13. I have discussed at length the different types of values held by human beings in *Caring: How Can We Love One Another* (Mahwah, New Jersey: Paulist Press, 1981), pp. 133-47. I have found the Myers-Briggs Personality Type Indicator (MBTI) the best tool in helping people understand how differently we look at the world. This instrument helps us to understand ourselves (all types are needed for a healthy society) and to see how much we need the other types. In addition, books on Values Clarification help us see that human beings have different priorities. Sincere Christians can have different values and respond in very different ways to the same situation. This understanding makes it *much easier to forgive other people.*

Loving Special Neighbors

1. Van der Post, *The Face Beside the Fire* (New York: William Morrow and Company, Inc., 1953), p. 34.

2. St. Ambrose, *Duties of the Clergy*, book 2, chapter 7, sections 37-38.

3. Louis Evely, *That Man Is You* (New York: Paulist Press, 1966), pp. 16 and 26.

4. This subject is discussed by Maxine Rock, *The Smithsonian*, March 1995, pp. 70-75.

5. My wife and I have collaborated on a book, Morton and Barbara Kelsey, *Sacrament of Sexuality* (New York: Continuum, 1995). In it we state our belief that sexuality can only be sacramental when it occurs between two people in a permanent relationship who are relating *as equals* and have a deep caring for each other, the kind of caring described by Paul in 1 Corinthians 13.

6. I have described the history of the unique Christian healing ministry in *Healing and Christianity* (Minneapolis, Minnesota: Augsburg, 1995). I have had the pleasure of lecturing for Cardinal Suenens in

Malines, Belgium, and discussing with him the importance of the healing ministry in churches today.

7. Van der Post, *The Face Beside the Fire*, p. 79.

8. Walter Wink, "Neither Passivity Nor Violence: Jesus' Third Way," *Forum* 7, 1991, pp. 5-28. His most complete study is *Engaging the Powers*, "Discernment and Resistance in a World of Domination" (Minneapolis, Minnesota: Fortress Press, 1992).

9. Pamphlet #96, *Gossip* (Pecos, New Mexico: Dove Publications, n.d.).

10. *The Collected Works of St. Teresa of Avila* (Washington, D.C.: ICS Publications, 1976), Vol. 1, *The Book of Her Life*, p. 92.

11. Dean Jahn has published widely on his careful studies in this field. This statement is found in *Princeton Alumni Weekly Special Report*, December 4, 1978.

12. Graham Greene, *The Heart of the Matter*, 1948; (reprinted New York: Penguin Books, 1978), p. 124.

13. The sections on loving the acquaintance, the enemy and the stranger draw heavily on chapters 9, 10 and 11 of *Caring: How Can We Love One Another?*

14. *Notre Dame Magazine*, Winter 1994-1995, Volume 23, Number 4, p. 78, George Howard, "The Lesser of Two Evils."

15. More information on this program can be obtained from Don McClanen, Ministry of Money, Two Professional Drive, Suite 220, Gaithersburg, Maryland 20879.

16. These reflections on our environment and money are drawn in part from my book, *Reaching: The Journey to Fulfillment* (Minneapolis, Minnesota: Augsburg, 1994), pp. 46-53.

The Invincible Power of Love

1. The following quotation is from Stanislav Grof, *Beyond the Brain: Birth, Death and Transcendence in Psychotherapy* (Albany, New York: State University of New York Press, 1985), p. 369.

"Particularly those who have experienced states of cosmic unity have an entirely new attitude toward the psychotherapeutic process. They have discovered a new, unexpected source of strength and their true identity. They now see their current life problems and past biographical material from a completely new perspective. From this new perspective, the events of their present existence do not seem to have the same overwhelming relevance that they had before. In addition, the goal of the psychological work is now clear; further self-exploration resembles the broadening and clearing of a road to a known destination, rather than blind digging in a dark tunnel."

Another relevant book is by Michael Washburn, *The Ego and the Dynamic Ground: A Transpersonal Theory of Human Development* (2d ed.) (Albany, New York: State University of New York Press, 1995).

Washburn's thesis in brief is that human development moves through pre-egoic and body egoic phases before developing the mental ego. The mental ego, which is considered by most psychologists as the end developmental state, in fact represents not only a stage of necessary development but also a separation from the dynamic ground. Midlife crises that succeed dissolve the centrality of the mental ego's project. Persons who go through further development experience "regression in service of the transcendent" and become "polymorphously sensual," that is, they reconnect with their bodies and with the dynamic ground; they become like "little children" but with a new and deeper connection to the dynamic ground, the life-giving source, God.

2. *Reaching: The Journey to Fulfillment* (Minneapolis: Augsburg Fortress, 1994), pp. 171-74 and 193-96.

3. Pinchas Lapide, *The Resurrection of Jesus: A Jewish Perspective* (Minneapolis, Minnesota: Augsburg, 1984), pp. 148-49.

4. Paul Tournier, *Creative Suffering* (San Francisco: Harper & Row, 1982).